From Riches to Rags

The Life of a Black Country Entrepreneur and Charity Fundraiser

Geoff Hill MBE

Hope you enjoy it!

Geoff Hill

SUTTON PUBLISHING

Sutton Publishing Limited
Phoenix Mill · Thrupp · Stroud
Gloucestershire · GL5 2BU

First published 2006

British Library Cataloguing in Publication Data
A catalogue record for this book is available from the British Library.

ISBN 0-7509-4459-5

All photographs from author's collection unless otherwise indicated.

Typeset in 10.5/13pt Galliard.
Typesetting and origination by
Sutton Publishing Limited.
Printed and bound in England by
J.H. Haynes & Co. Ltd, Sparkford.

Contents

THE BLACK COUNTRY SOCIETY

The Black Country Society is proud to be associated with **Sutton Publishing** of Stroud. In 1994 the society was invited by Sutton Publishing to collaborate in what has proved to be a highly successful publishing partnership, namely the extension of the *Britain in Old Photographs* series into the Black Country. In this joint venture the Black Country Society has played an important role in establishing and developing a major contribution to the region's photographic archives by encouraging society members to compile books of photographs of the area or town in which they live.

The first book in the Black Country series was *Wednesbury in Old Photographs* by Ian Bott, launched by Lord Archer of Sandwell in November 1994. Since then almost 70 Black Country titles have been published. The total number of photographs contained in these books is in excess of 13,000, suggesting that the whole collection is probably the largest regional photographic survey of its type in any part of the country to date.

This voluntary society was founded in 1967 as a reaction to the trends of the late 1950s and early '60s. This was a time when the reorganisation of local government was seen as a threat to the identity of individual communities and when, in the name of progress and modernisation, the industrial heritage of the Black Country was in danger of being swept away.

The general aims of the society are to stimulate interest in the past, present and future of the Black Country, and to secure at regional and national levels an accurate understanding and portrayal of what constitutes the Black Country and, wherever possible, to encourage and facilitate the preservation of the Black Country's heritage.

The society, which now has over 2,500 members worldwide, organises a yearly programme of activities. There are six venues in the Black Country where evening meetings are held on a monthly basis from September to April. In the summer months, there are fortnightly guided evening walks in the Black Country and its green borderland, and there is also a full programme of excursions further afield by car. Details of all these activities are to be found on the society's website, **www.blackcountrysociety.co.uk**, and in *The Blackcountryman*, the quarterly magazine that is distributed to all members.

PO Box 71 · Kingswinford · West Midlands DY6 9YN

Foreword

Several people have asked me when I first started writing my autobiography. It was, in fact, only after I had finished my long session at Mary Stevens Hospice in August 2002 that I suddenly had time to do other things in my life than fundraising. Most of the time, it was a mere hour here and there scribbling down notes as I thought that it would only ever be read in years to come by friends and family.

It was only in 2005 that an old friend of mine from school days, Stan Hill, kindly 'fine tuned' it for me, ready for publication. Stan is a retired headmaster with a wealth of writing experience as a past editor of *The Blackcountryman* and also an author of several Black Country books. It was he who broke the news to me that a reputable firm, Sutton Publishing, was interested in publishing my memoirs – much to my surprise.

It was then that I wondered how I could turn the sale of the book into a fundraising event, and decided to buy 1,000 copies so that six of my favourite charities would each benefit by the money that I raise from the sale of them. The charities are:

Mary Stevens Hospice
Stourbridge Age Concern
Dudley Hope Trust
The Leukaemia Unit Appeal Fund
Sunfield Childrens' Home
Action Heart, Russells Hall

Royalties from further sales will go to the Geoff Hill Charitable Trust to help needy groups and charities in the local area.

As I shall be 79 by book-launch day it may well be my last major fundraising event. But, knowing me, who knows? There may still be a little life in the old dog yet!

Geoff Hill
2006

Introduction

It was 30 June 1992; more importantly, it was my 65th birthday. My dear wife, Sue, had insisted on throwing a party for me, inviting, so I thought, just fifteen to twenty close friends. Unusually for Sue (who always did her own cooking for parties), she had thought that it might be nice to have an outside caterer in for a change, so that she could relax and help to look after the guests. We had an Enville Golf Club friend, Freddie de Freitas, who ran a very good restaurant in Stourbridge and Sue soon had him organised to do whatever was required on the night.

At about 7.30 p.m. friends began to arrive, congratulating me and giving presents. Then, when most were there, I happened to look out from the back terrace towards the road and saw quite a number of cars. On my enquiring what could be happening, someone said, 'Oh, I think there's a sponsored walk starting from here tonight.' Foolishly, I believed it!

About 20 minutes later all hell seemed to break loose when a marching band playing at full blast came strutting down the side lawn, followed by some fifty more surprise guests who had been quietly gathering in my neighbour's drive! It was a wonderful surprise, and so typical of Sue.

For some time I was at a loss for words. People I had not seen for years were mingling with others to whom I had been talking only earlier that day! The weather

The 'From Riches to Rags'
65th birthday cake,
30 June 1992.

The marching band at Geoff's surprise birthday party on 30 June 1992.

was kind and it became a lovely, memorable evening in the company of friends from the golf club, business and the more recent Hospice fundraising.

Food and drinks were served and eventually Sue brought out a gorgeous birthday cake which one of my staff had made. On the top of the cake was a very good reproduction of the Geoff Hill Electrical Store in brown and cream, with a long canopy over the shop windows. At the bottom of the cake was an equally good reproduction, in blue and white, of the Mary Stevens Hospice shop at Stourbridge, which I had not long ago opened. The writing on the cake said simply, 'From Riches', alongside the Geoff Hill shop and, 'To Rags', alongside the Hospice shop! It was only on later reflection that I realised how these four simple words seemed totally to encapsulate my whole working life. The first forty-five years were dedicated to the 'Riches' stage and the last fifteen years to the 'Rags' phase of my life, which, although always of a charitable nature, was just as diverse and time consuming as the former. I had always relished a challenge!

But the birthday party was by no means over, although I had thought so at the time. There was still one more surprise up Sue's sleeve: that came at about 11 p.m. when Mike Sanchez arrived. Mike was a keyboard player/vocalist who performed around the local night-clubs and was one of my son Nigel's favourite performers. He set his keyboard up in the dining hall and when everyone was packed in on chairs, on the floor and up the open-plan staircase, he burst into song. Mike was so good there was no way we were going to let him go until the early hours. It was some birthday party!

1

Early Years

It all started on 30 June 1927, when I was born in a small terraced house at 36 Trinity Street, Brierley Hill; the son of James Alfred Hill, manager of the invoice department at Round Oak Steel Works, Brierley Hill, and Ada Hill, his wife. I had a sister named Nellie May (later to be known as Gerry), who was nearly 5 years old at the time.

The house was typical of many pre-war houses: two rooms and a kitchen downstairs and three bedrooms upstairs, one of which was a single room. The only toilet was outside and bath nights were once a week, using a large tin bath in front of the old black-leaded grate, with water baled out of a coal-fired boiler in the kitchen. I never looked forward to bath nights. The worst part for me was when it came to hair-washing time, when I inevitably ended up with soap in my eyes, followed by dad's most vigorous hair rub with a rough towel. Dad rubbed it so hard I am sure my scalp 'glowed' afterwards. I was not a happy little boy on those occasions!

My father had quite a responsible job. In the early war years he would often work over until about 8 p.m., because he was both short of staff and badly paid, as were most office personnel in those days. This meant that things at home had to be taken care of and made to last. So presents and clothes were kept to a minimum, but were nevertheless usually of good quality.

One present of my own choice was allowed at birthdays and Christmas. I can remember so well a farmyard set of animals, a fort with lead soldiers and, probably my favourite plaything, a lovely polished wooden bagatelle pintable with chrome

Geoff on a donkey with his sister during a holiday at Blackpool.

balls. For many years this was my most treasured possession and was carefully placed back in its original cardboard box every time after use. I can remember on one occasion my young cousin, Barbara, came to visit us with her mother and I was told to let her play with my treasured bagatelle table. I very nearly dug my heels in and refused to let her even touch it.

Games were simple in those days and often made up. I know that I played hop-scotch quite a lot, which was simply chalking up some numbered squares in the road, then having to hop on one leg while pushing a small square of wood from one square to the next. I also remember that there were cast-iron railings on the wall outside our front-room window. I would stand for hours trying to lasso the spikes of the railings, pretending I was Tom Mix, the western cowboy hero of the time, lassoing cattle. Marbles were another attraction and lots of different games could be invented with those little glass spheres; even racing them down the sloping garden path would while away an hour or two.

Our little treat in those days was a Sunday bus ride two or three times a year to either Clent or Kinver. If we were extremely lucky we might get a week's holiday at Weston-super-Mare or Blackpool.

My father was a keen gardener and as I grew older I was able to help him by doing odd jobs. There was a time I kept rabbits, until they burrowed under the fence at the bottom of the garden and got into the allotments on the other

Left: Geoff and his sister outside the aviary containing his beloved budgerigars.
Right: Geoff's home at 36 Trinity Street, Brierley Hill, as it is today.

Geoff's father, Alfred Hill.   *Geoff's mother, Ada Hill.*

side, where they nibbled away to their hearts' content at the vegetables being grown there!

When I was still quite young I used to run errands for the local people, often for the lady who kept the little corner shop across the road. 'Run' was the operative word because I would love to race the quarter mile or so along the length of Trinity Street, up Talbot Street to the shops, get served as quickly as possible, then run all the way back. All this just to hear the grateful recipient say, 'You've never possibly done the shopping already, Geoffrey?' People would often want to give me a penny or a halfpenny for my trouble but I always refused to take it. However, the lady at the corner shop sold sweets and if she gave me some of those I found it quite impossible to refuse.

As I grew older I had a passion for budgerigars. My father, who was a very good carpenter, built me a wonderful aviary that spanned the whole width of our garden. Soon I acquired a selection of pairs of the yellow, green and blue varieties. I then had a lot of pleasure from breeding and selling the offspring, but unfortunately when war broke out the imported food eventually became unobtainable. The sad outcome was that one day I had to open the flight doors and let them all fly away.

While mentioning the war, I must relate the happenings on one horrendous night in 1944. I was sleeping in the front bedroom with my father when, in the middle of the night, there was suddenly one almighty crash that sounded as though a bomb had hit us, and the bedroom windows were blown in. In actual fact it was one of our own damaged planes returning from a bombing mission over Germany. The flight

The Earl of Dudley's Round Oak Works staff photograph, 1937. Geoff's father is in the second row from the back, fourth from the right. (Black Country Bugle)

At 3.30 a.m. on 16 March 1944 a Halifax Mk 3 bomber, NLW 413, returning from a raid on Germany, crashed onto houses in Adelaide Street only 80yd from Geoff's home in Trinity Street. This photograph shows the devastation caused. One person was killed. (Express & Star)

crew had all baled out and the pilotless Halifax bomber flew on, before ploughing through gardens and into a row of terraced houses in Adelaide Street, just yards away across the road from us. Several houses were badly damaged and one or two had to be completely rebuilt. Fortunately, only one person lost her life, a lady staying with her parents for the weekend. Ironically, her husband was serving in the RAF at the time.

2

School Days

The early years soon passed, and when I was 5 years old it was time to start school. My mother took me along to Bent Street Infants' School in Brierley Hill, and I seemed to settle into this new regime quite easily. In fact, my mother only took me on the first day because I insisted on going by myself afterwards – something which would be almost impossible today with the growth of traffic and other hazards for young children. Going on my own did not last for long because, I remember, I soon acquired two girlfriends, collecting them from their homes in the next street for us to go off happily to school as a threesome.

School work came fairly easily to me and I soon became familiar with being top or top but one in examinations. The subject that I excelled in was arithmetic, and it has remained that way throughout my life. I can remember on one occasion having to go over to the Senior School on the same site, presumably to shame the much older pupils there into working harder. I was asked and answered several mental arithmetic problems that the older boys were struggling with.

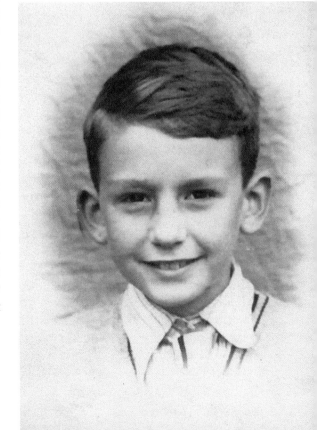

The years went by and I was soon to transfer to my next school, which was a similar distance away but in the opposite direction, at Brockmoor. I soon settled in there, managing to stay at or near the top of each class. The pinnacle of my whole scholastic career came in my final year, when I was an 11-year-old in Mr Jones's class. It was checking-out time and all seven subjects in our end-of-term exams had been marked and returned by the teachers. I remember Mr Jones drew up his portly frame in front of his desk and said, 'Right, class, now let's see who's come out top?' Straight

An early school photograph taken at Brockmoor Junior Mixed School.

Bent Street Infants' School, Brierley Hill, with Bent Street Senior Boys' School in the background.

away the rest of the class chanted, 'Geoffrey Hill, sir!' 'What makes you think you are top, Hill?' demanded Mr Jones. 'Well, nobody could have beaten me,' I replied, 'because I happen to have got ten marks out of ten in all seven subjects.'

Mr Jones was quite obviously surprised and muttered something about it never having happened before in his career; which was quite something for him to admit, because he was a teacher feared by most pupils and very adept at using the cane. Unfortunately, this moment of scholastic genius was not to last, as I was soon to pass the exam which would enable me to go to King Edward's Grammar School, Stourbridge – there to encounter the bane of my life, homework! 'The Grammar School' as it was known really was a beautiful school to attend; unfortunately, at that time I never fully appreciated the wonderful surroundings and opportunities it presented.

New entrants all started in the third form, of which there were three classes: 3.1, 3.2 and 3.3. I was allocated to 3.2, which was actually housed in what was known as 'the tin tabernacle'. This was like an oversized Nissen hut and situated in the playground area. It was of an all-corrugated-sheet construction and had a coal-fired boiler for heating during the winter months. I remember that when the less strict masters or mistresses were taking class, some of the naughty boys would slip their erasers onto the boiler, resulting shortly afterwards in a horrendous stench filling the room. Needless to say, no one would own up and as a result it would sometimes end in the whole class being punished with detention.

At the end of the first year, the top third of each of the three classes were merged into a class called 4.1, instead of going into a Lower Fourth followed by an Upper Fourth class the following year. This meant that two years' school work had to be crammed into one year, with the result that we would take the School Certificate Examination at 15, instead of 16.

It was during this period that I bought my first bike from a fellow schoolboy for the grand price of 10s. It was a fairly old and quite heavy touring bike with semi-dropped handlebars, but it soon became my pride and joy. I went to school on it for quite some time but can remember occasions when I would be obliged to go on the bus. If I had been out cycling the previous evening and had not done my homework, I would have to try and complete it on the bus ride into Stourbridge!

While I was at school I joined the Army Cadets, wearing the thick khaki uniform and heavy boots, along with puttees around my legs. It was a uniform that very nearly cost me my life, because I had an unforgettable experience while we were

Brockmoor Junior Mixed School.

away at camp by the riverside near Arley. Some Sea Cadets in an adjacent field had been using light kayak boats on the river and had left one on the riverbank. My friend and I spotted it and, as no one was about, thought we would have a quick go in it on the river. We had just about reached the middle when we noticed water building up at quite an alarming rate in the bottom of the boat, and immediately realised that it must have had a leak and had been left on the bank on purpose to dry out for repair. Quite soon the boat filled with water and sank, and we were in the river. There appeared to be no imminent danger because it was only chest deep. My friend immediately made his way towards the bank, but I foolishly tried to chase after the boat, which had now started floating downstream. Almost at once I found myself in much deeper water and, because of my heavy clothes and boots, quite incapable of swimming. Suddenly, I was sinking to the bottom of the river, then pushing back again to break surface and shout for help. I don't know how many times I did this, but it seemed an eternity. Just as I was nearing complete exhaustion I noticed a man swimming furiously towards me; seconds later he had me in his arms. 'Don't struggle,' he said, as he got me over onto my back with my head held out of the water. I certainly had no energy left in my body to struggle. We were some distance downstream and the current was quite strong; my rescuer had to ease his way against it while swimming back to the bank with me. However, in just a few minutes he had me over to the riverbank in a state of utter exhaustion. I was carried back to my tent, where I slept for several hours before they were able to transport me back home. I never knew who my rescuer was, but I know that I would never have survived the day had it not been for his swift, life-saving action.

At King Edward's the sports were cricket and rugby, instead of the football that I had been used to. I never took to rugby, although I quite liked cricket and was a reasonably good bowler, but I found the time spent fielding somewhat boring. However, later in my working life I did have the opportunity to play a few games of competitive cricket, which I quite enjoyed.

My first year at school flew by. I was now in the fourth form, which was an entirely different proposition because it was composed of the top one-third of each of the third forms: quite a brainy bunch of boys. I soon started to drop down towards the bottom half of the class, particularly as I was not giving the time to homework that I should, mainly due to my increasing interest in cycling. I would be off on my bike most summer evenings, often doing 40 miles or so. When I eventually bought a cyclometer to record the mileage covered, I could not rest until I had cycled 100 miles in a day!

Lower and Upper Fifth forms followed, but I was anxious to get out into the big, wide world and see what work I could find. I eventually persuaded my father to agree to speak to the headmaster. The outcome was that I was allowed to leave school at the age of 15, instead of 16.

I have glossed over my early years without mentioning the one big tragedy of that formative time, the death of my dear mother ten years to the day after she had given birth to me. As my sister was particularly close to my father, so was I to my mother. For some six months before she died my father knew that the cancer she had would eventually lead to her death. I was only 9 at the time and was sheltered from the serious nature of her illness; at the time of her death I was moved away for a day or two, only to be told the dreadful news later. With my sister being only 14, we had to have a help come to clean the house. I remember we had one or two disasters before we found a suitable one, but things were never quite the same again.

My sister was still at Dudley Girls' High School and father had little money for holidays. As we all liked the country, he found a farm on Bromyard Downs that took in boarders. We would catch a bus to Stourbridge, another to Worcester, then one to Bromyard, reversing the process to come home. A brother and sister ran the farm. Some years later she was to marry my father and they eventually had a son, my stepbrother Robert, who was some twenty years younger than me.

Before my father married Bet – a rather quiet and very countrified lady – we had decided that it might be time to move from our rather small terraced home in Trinity Street. One day I noticed on the display board next to Knott's the Butcher in the High Street, an advert that looked quite interesting. A couple whose daughter, Betty Emery, was quite a famous singer on stage in London, were looking for a smaller place than the house in which they were living. Their house was called The Gables and stood high up from the road, right opposite the railway station, and seemed a very imposing residence after our quite humble abode. With its large reception rooms downstairs, a lovely open stairway led from the hall up to a landing with three bedrooms leading off it and, the icing on the cake, a beautiful bathroom! The elderly couple seemed quite happy to move into our house: a week or two later it all took place.

My sister, meanwhile, had grown into a very attractive young lady. During the war years I remember a succession of callers who came knocking on our back door. Mainly Air Force men based at Halfpenny Green Airport, they included Yanks, Canadians, New Zealanders, Australians and one guy in particular from a place called Uruguay in South America. His name was Colin Fairless and he was to become the one that my sister chose as her husband. After the war, she boarded a freight ship for the three-week voyage to South America. There she married, had two sons, and has spent a very happy life.

3

My Pre-call-up Jobs

As soon as I knew that I was going to be able to leave school a year early, I started looking for my first job, managing to obtain one as an assistant to the storekeeper at Prestwood Sanatorium, which in those days was for male tuberculosis patients. The premises consisted of the main block of offices, stores and staff quarters. For the patients there were four long, open-fronted wards on a sloping hillside some 30yd away. The wards were open-fronted because fresh air was part of the cure for tuberculosis.

My work there was to assist the storekeeper, Jim, by checking in all goods and provisions, then putting them together as required for either the kitchen or wards. It was now wartime and my first recollection was one of shock to see such large quantities of food, most of which was rationed to a few ounces per week. Another attraction, which it did not take me long to come to terms with, was that seventy nurses and maids worked there, along with about half a dozen male staff.

I very soon began to enjoy work much more than school and homework; I was also earning the princely sum of £2 10s per week. There was quite a good social side too. As it was quite a distance from Stourbridge, many of the nurses and maids had live-in quarters, and this meant that, by and large, they had to make their own entertainment. Occasionally they would arrange a dance in the large hall, where I especially liked the 'mixed tag' quicksteps and would often have a small queue of girls waiting to 'tag' me!

The army had taken over Enville Hall, which was only 2 or 3 miles away. One night they arranged a big dance there with a proper band instead of the records that we used to play. The army boys needed some girls to dance with: where else but to find them than at Prestwood Sanatorium? The night arrived and two large army trucks rolled up. All the girls were dressed in their finery, except for the unfortunate ones who were on duty that night. They were all being given a 'leg up' by the men into the backs of the trucks, when suddenly the men doing this had quite a shock, finding themselves lifting me in as well. The girls knew I was a very keen dancer and they all seemed quite happy to have me along too. I remember it being a great night with lots to eat and drink, and particularly great fun coming back afterwards in the back of the truck with all those girls to look after!

I had been at the sanatorium about twelve months and was probably just about 16, when I became attracted to the very good-looking assistant cook. After a time she became so attached to me that she broke off her engagement to the son of the sanatorium's resident engineer. We had been out for a few walks and to the pictures at Stourbridge, and had one particular night gone for a walk alongside the canal that ran just a few hundred yards away. We had stopped under one of the arches when she started talking seriously about our relationship together, telling me that she was 19 and asked me:

'Are you nineteen, Geoff?'

'No, not yet,' I replied, hesitantly.

'Eighteen, then, I suppose?'

'Not yet,' I replied, even more hesitantly.

'Seventeen, then?' she said, with astonishment in her tone.

'No,' I said very feebly.

'You're only sixteen?' she stammered out.

'I'm afraid so!' I said apologetically.

That was the end of our relationship. Not long afterwards she was re-engaged to her old boyfriend and I believe they married soon after.

Much as I enjoyed my stay at Prestwood, after about eighteen months I realised that the future was rather limited there and I longed for pastures new. I had already enrolled at Dudley Technical College, taking a Royal Society of Arts evening course in accountancy, so I applied for and was successful in obtaining a bookkeeping job at the Black Country chain-making firm, Eliza Tinsley of Old Hill.

It was a very old-established firm, certainly giving that impression from the moment I arrived there. The desks were the 'stand-up' ones and looked from their gnarled appearance as though they must have dated back to Victorian times. When I went round the outbuildings where the chains were made everything seemed to be done by hand, with lots of furnaces, banging and welding. I believe also that teams of outworkers were still making a considerable amount of chain at home. The two bosses, who were by then well into their middle age, were still referred to as Master George and Master John – certainly shades of years gone by.

After a few months working there I managed to pass my accountancy examination at Dudley Technical College and again started looking around for a job to practise my new bookkeeping skills. I finally landed a job as an audit clerk working for a very small practice based in Dudley High Street, run by a very old chartered accountant named Arnold T. Stevenson. By small, I mean that, apart from a young secretary, the only other person there was a man in his forties who had worked for him for more than twenty years, and whom I was about to replace.

I was very soon on a steep learning curve, having to go out to do the audit on my own; except for the compilation of the final balance sheets and tax returns etc. which Mr Stevenson himself undertook. It was certainly a long way removed from the carefree days I had spent only a few months previously at Prestwood Sanatorium. I can remember doing an audit for a Mutual Society in Dudley, when one of the many young girls in the office moved a filing cabinet to expose an old two-pin 15-amp socket. 'I wonder if it works,' she said. 'It would be great to boil the kettle on if it does.' I looked at the two metal-nibbed pens on the desk, and said, 'I'll test it for you if you like.'

With a pen in each hand, I crossed the metal holders over each other and pushed the nibs into the socket. There was a flash and loud bang. All that was left at the end of each pen was a blob of solder! Both nibs had disintegrated, and as the one pen was Mr Stevenson's favourite, with a mother-of-pearl handle, I was really in the doghouse when he found out. Worse was to come, because it was the time when fire-watchers had to be on duty at night in case of incendiary bombs. Unfortunately it happened to be the manager's turn that evening and not until he turned up at 10 p.m. did he discover that I must have also blown a main fuse – meaning that there were neither heat nor hot drinks that night! It was my first practical lesson in electricity, and one I never forgot!

Dudley was a very good shopping centre in those days and I had to do the audit for many of the shops there, including the very good-quality and privately owned ladies' and gentlemen's outfitters. I remember being surprised at how much profit margin these high-class shops made on clothes, making a mental note then that it might be an area to think of moving into, as and when finance and circumstances were appropriate.

Twelve months or so went by and I was approaching my call-up for mobilisation at the age of 18. One day Mr Stevenson called me into his office and said that he was intending to lodge an appeal against my call-up, on the grounds that his business was reliant on my services. It would certainly not be easy for him to get a replacement for me, as most of the able-bodied men of 18 and over had been called for National Service. I thought it over for a while, finally deciding that long-term audit clerking was too uninspiring a job for me anyway, so I put my notice in straight away.

My cycle racing had taken off big-time by then and I was able to spend a few very interesting months working for the famous racing cyclist Percy Stallard, who had a shop in Broad Street, Wolverhampton. It was a very popular shop, attracting racing cyclists from a wide area. He had his own racing frames made so that complete Percy Stallard racing bikes could be assembled on the premises. My job was to look after the shop while Percy was in the workshop. Occasionally, he would bring me in a wheel to build. This was done by threading the spokes through the hub and outer rim, then spinning the wheel around on a stand and adjusting the tension on each spoke until it spun perfectly true.

I had been a member of Wolverhampton Racing Club for some time. The club, together with Wolverhampton Wheelers, meant that well over 100 racing cyclists were dropping into the shop on a regular basis for spares and a chat; it was the sort of job that I hardly needed to be paid to do! On top of this, it was 10 miles or so from Brierley Hill to Wolverhampton; as I cycled there and back each day, usually at speed, it kept me in pretty good condition, even before starting to go out on evening training runs.

Percy was quite a character in the cycle racing world and was actually responsible for originating massed-start road racing in this country. The first race was held from Llangollen to Wolverhampton, only a year or two before I started to work for him. He also changed the whole concept of cycle racing, because the individual time trial had usually been held early morning before much traffic was on the roads and contestants wore dark tops and black tights! Massed-start riders turned out in shorts, with brightly coloured jerseys in their individual team colours, just as you see them on the roads today or competing in the Tour de France. The start and finish of races are now often held in town centres instead of a quite road somewhere in the country.

Much as I enjoyed working for Percy Stallard it was all too good to last; after a few months I was 18 and due for call-up. My original intention was to apply to join the RAF, but there was a national shortage of miners, as most of the adult males were in the different branches of the armed forces. Therefore, as it was only two months before the end of the war, I conscripted to join the 'Bevin Boys' as they were then called. This way I would spend my time helping to produce the nation's coal and still carry on with my cycle racing!

4

My Cycle-racing Days

During my teenage years, as well as being dedicated to my road to riches during working hours, I very soon became just as dedicated to my cycling and cycle racing.

It all started when I joined a cycling club called the Audnam Wheelers that met – coincidentally enough – just round the corner from the place in Brettell Lane where I was to start my electrical retailing store some 16 or 17 years later. I was about 15 years old at the time.

Audnam Wheelers' members were really just very nice people of all ages who met every Sunday morning to go for a social spin on their bikes into some of our wonderful countryside. There were, however, one or two of the more energetic and younger fraternity who fancied racing, and I seem to remember that we had one or two 10-mile time trials, my first experience of competitive racing.

It was around this time that I would go off on long cycle rides, sometimes with others, sometimes alone, that astounded my poor sister and father when I returned home. I remember that once I cycled off, with two older friends, up to the Lake District; after spending a whole day cycling round the lakes we decided to cycle through the night so that we could have a day at Blackpool on the way home. Unfortunately, our plan went horribly wrong when one of the lads decided, around midnight, that he wasn't going to make it; so we decided to see if we could find somewhere to sleep. Eventually we saw a farm with a light still on. In answer to our enquiry if there was anywhere we could stay the night, the good news was that the farmer said the three of us could sleep in the cow-shed. The bad news was that he would have to get us out at 6 a.m. to milk the cows! The next day we continued on to Blackpool for an hour or two on the front before starting the long ride home.

A year or two later I had another unfortunate incident in the Lake District when I bought an old pre-war touring tandem and went there with my girlfriend, Lorraine Jackson, on the back. We were staying in a Youth Hostel high up, overlooking one of the lakes. I went out the following morning to collect the tandem from the bike-shed and bring it round to the front of the building ready for Lorraine to join me for our departure. She had been settling our account at the front desk and turned to come out to where I was standing in bright sunshine. Not realising that there was a heavy glass door between us, she walked straight into it, cutting her knee quite badly. The warden of the hostel rushed us down to the nearest town where a doctor put several stitches in and bound up the leg so that it was rigid. What was I to do? As we had only just arrived in the Lake District, I did not relish getting onto a train

Geoff winning the British League of Racing Cyclists' Junior Time Trial Championship, 1944. (Hart Photography Ltd)

and wending my way disconsolately home. What I ultimately decided to do was to knock the 'cotter pin' out of one pedal crank so that Lorraine was cycling on the back of the tandem with only one leg going round! We looked an odd combination, me having to push like hell to get up the Lakeland mountain passes, while my dear girlfriend sat serenely on the back pushing only one pedal. Needless to say, when we stopped it was Lorraine who got all the sympathy from people, not Joe Soap on the front who was doing all the extra work!

Later on there were times when I would cycle to work at Hilton Main Colliery on the tandem on my own, especially in the racing season. It certainly got me fit; it was fantastic to jump onto a lightweight racing bike at night after the 30-mile daytime slog on the tandem.

It was not long before I made contact with the Wolverhampton Racing Club and I couldn't wait to join one of the top cycle-racing clubs in the area. I soon settled in with this large group of dedicated racing cyclists and was regularly off to races at weekends in various parts of the country.

Even our Sunday club runs were often races in miniature, with the dedicated finish to the race usually being the 30mph sign of a town some 50 or 60 miles away.

We even went as far as Rhyl in North Wales and back in a day – a distance of some 200 miles from Brierley Hill!

I always remember a club run that we had to Ross-on-Wye when Percy Stallard and I, both being good hill climbers, broke away over the Malvern Hills and, as was the custom, took it in turns to 'break the wind'. On getting through Ledbury, however, still with 10 miles to go, I pulled over slightly and turned around to see Percy with his mouth open and his head rolling from side to side, obviously in no state to set the pace for us. I pulled over to check Percy a few more times before we reached Ross-on-Wye and each time he still looked absolutely exhausted. It was only when we turned a corner and the 30mph sign was just 100yd away that Percy suddenly flashed past me with a gigantic grin on his face, then threw his arms in the air as he charged past the finishing post! He was quite a character, was Percy.

I soon started to improve and to win the odd small race, while finishing among the leaders in the larger events.

The pinnacle of my cycling career arrived in 1944 when I was 17 and managed to win the British League of Racing Cyclists' Junior Time Trial Championship over 40 miles at Barnet in north London. It came as quite a surprise to everyone, as Don Welch, a very good young racing cyclist over from America, had been winning most of the junior events that year and was heavily fancied to win this championship.

Later that year we were to have the first multi-stage massed-start race to be held in this country, the Brighton to Glasgow Cycle Race, over six daily stages with stops at London, Wolverhampton, Bradford, Newcastle, Edinburgh and finally Glasgow.

The start of the Anglo-Dutch International Road Race at Tilburg, Holland, 1946. Geoff with mop of dark hair is at the centre of the picture.

Geoff winning the 25-mile time trial, Stafford, 1946.

I went down to London on the train with a team from the Wolverhampton Racing Club, then we all cycled down to Brighton to the bed-and-breakfast place where we were to stay the night. I had had a bad throat for a few days and the next morning it seemed to be much worse, so I asked the landlady if there was a chemist's shop handy.

'You pass the hospital on the way down to the start,' the landlady replied, 'I should pop in there if I were you and get it seen to properly.'

I did as she recommended and told the rest of the lads that I would see them down at the changing rooms before the start.

Imagine my surprise only a few minutes later when the doctor, who examined me in the outpatients' facility, pronounced that he thought I could have diphtheria and was sending me off to an isolation hospital in an ambulance right away! One minute I had been expecting to start an arduous 568-mile race over three mountain passes, now I was lying on my back on a stretcher in the back of an ambulance. After a few days they were able to diagnose a very bad quinsy throat, and not diphtheria, but I was still kept there for 10 days or so and then had to cycle all the way home from Brighton on my own, after having been immobile for the whole period.

I must confess that my stay in hospital was not as bad as it sounds, because I had a rather gorgeous young nurse looking after me. After a few days, when I was starting

Geoff, after winning the Dudley Circuit Time Trial, March 1946. His sister is on the left of the picture.

to feel better, she would bring me a hot drink at night, put the screens round and sit on the side of my bed for a chat. All I can remember now is that she lived near Kew Gardens and that she had a wonderful bedside manner.

Later in the year I was to have a very interesting week at Tilburg in Holland, when I came third in an international race watched by some 20,000 people. We also raced in Belgium and I was doing quite well, winning the Sprint Prize early in the race, but we soon made our first contact with the notorious Belgian cobbles that vibrated your whole body as you rode over them on the small, high-pressure tyres with which our bikes were fitted. Over there, European riders were using much larger tyres that cushioned the vibration. Needless to say, unfortunately I didn't finish that race.

I started 1946 by winning the first three races of the year and was really striking top form. The first was a really tough, massed-start race, called the Nidderdale Road Race, round a very hilly course in Yorkshire, where I broke the course record by over 4 minutes, winning in a close sprint from the Scottish champion, Alex Hendry. The second race was a 25-mile time trial at Stafford that I won by just over a minute. The third win was a surprise even to me, because I beat the national time-trial champion, Ted Jones, into second place by nearly 2 minutes, with the national road-race champion, Ernie Clements, a minute further away in third place. This race took place locally on a circuit starting from Dudley and was probably one of the best performances of my career.

Later in the year I was to head the first 'independent' category cycle-racing team in the country. There were no professional cycle races here in those days, and the independent category was introduced as a stepping-stone to a professional racing circuit. It meant that for a limited period of time I was able to earn up to £5 per race instead of prizes; also, that I could earn an additional £5 per race in sponsorship. Once the period of time expired I would have to return to amateur status or turn professional.

I had by then transferred to the Dudley Castle Cycling Club and was racing under the sponsorship of Hickman Cycles, which was a retail cycle-racing shop based in King Street, Dudley. Our first race was to be the Brighton to Glasgow six-day race, which was in later years to become the Tour of Britain Road Race. I was joined in the team by two other prominent racing cyclists, Arthur Stakehouse and Jim Pryer.

After a wonderful send-off on the Promenade by the Mayor of Brighton, I settled down with some eighty other racing cyclists to tackle the first, reasonably short, stage to London. I couldn't have had a better start, because after only 30 miles I

Geoff, the fifth racing cyclist from the right, behind Percy Stallard and Bobby Thom, 1946. Thom later became the manager of the Great Britain team.

Geoff, after winning the Cyclo-Cross Race from Horace Poole and Ben Whitmore, 1946.

managed to win the first 'hill climb' at Redhill in Surrey. Hill climbs are in effect a race within a race, usually on one, possibly two, severe climbs during each daily stage. As I was good at hill climbing I always relished the all-out sustained challenge of climbing a severe gradient of 1 or 2 miles at a flat-out speed. We finished the stage at London on a proper outdoor cycle track; in the final sprint I came in fourth.

The second stage was to be much more arduous, some 150 miles from central London, up the A5, to just south of Lichfield, then down through Walsall to finish in West Park, Wolverhampton. I was very pleased with my first day's ride and determined to try to stay in any leading breakaway groups so that I could finish the stage in contention for leadership. Things went well for the first 100 miles or so; I was in the leading group of a dozen or so when disaster struck and I had a puncture.

These days, with sophisticated equipment and back-up vehicles, it would only take seconds to change a wheel or even a whole bicycle, but in those days, still using pre-war equipment, it meant a several minutes' delay. To make matters worse, when I turned south from the A5 towards Walsall I was facing a strong head wind with no protection from other cyclists. Strong as I was in those days, even I was feeling the effects of the 130 or so miles of competitive racing already behind me. I eventually arrived at the finish in Wolverhampton some 17 minutes behind the winner and had effectively ruled myself out of a high finish at the end of the race.

My father never drove (most people didn't in those days), but I had an uncle who was in business and he drove my father and other friends all the way up to Buxton in Derbyshire. They also followed us on the next stage, to Bradford, the following day. I did quite well on that stage, and the next one to Newcastle, which was quite hilly. Then, on the following stage, which included steep climbs (which suited me), we crossed the border into Scotland and on to a big finish in Edinburgh. I had got myself into the top ten by then and was hoping to give it my best shot on the shorter and flatter stage to Glasgow, but fate stepped in again. I had another puncture, which I managed to rectify without too much loss of time on the leading bunch and finished the overall race in eleventh position.

In September 2004, Sue and I drove up to Bakewell in Derbyshire to see the start of the third stage of the Tour of Britain Cycle Race, which was being reinstated after a five-year break. I found it fascinating to compare the bikes, clothes and general razzmatazz of the official start, with large numbers of service vehicles in attendance, with the austere postwar race that I had competed in some fifty-eight years earlier. Coincidentally, I had raced through Buxton on our third stage of the race, which is just 12 miles down the road from Bakewell.

In October 1946 I was able to ride in an international race at Navan in Ireland. I had never been a particularly good traveller and was facing a long sea crossing for the first time – and it was a rough one! Consequently, I arrived at Dublin Mansion House for a reception by the Lord Mayor of Dublin in a rather fragile state. Even more important at the time was the following morning, when I was presented with a great big mixed grill for breakfast which looked absolutely delicious to a growing lad deprived of such sights because of the war years. My stomach was, however, still too delicate for such niceties and I remember I had to settle for a couple of pieces of dry toast. Fortunately, we had a couple of days to settle down before the big race and by the time the flag went down I was in pretty good shape again. After a great race several times round a country circuit, I eventually finished third to two extremely good Australian champions named Strom and Arnold. It was only when I arrived home a few days later that I found out I had made the headlines, having been billed as the leading English racing cyclist in the race.

I have another unusual cycling incident to report from 1946, when I competed in a hill climb at Ironbridge, Shropshire, up Madeley Bank as it was known, being the main road out of the town towards Madeley. We had set off at 1-minute intervals, but on the way down afterwards I was suddenly confronted with a long line of traffic. I pulled out and started pedalling like mad because I was riding on a very low fixed gear for the hill climb, and proceeded to shoot past the line of slow-moving traffic. It was only when I got level with the leading car, when it was too late to slow down, that I noticed to my horror that it was a police car! Some 10 minutes later I was back in the changing rooms when a policeman appeared and started to look at all our numbers. I remember sitting on mine, but it was to no avail and he eventually recognised me as the speeding cyclist. I got an appropriate telling-off and was told that I would be reported to the Chief Inspector of Shrewsbury. I was on tenterhooks for the next couple of weeks, wondering what action they would take against me, but I eventually received a letter of warning with indications that if it happened again I would be prosecuted. I sometimes wondered afterwards if it might have been good for my image – and certainly unusual – if, as a racing cyclist, I had been summoned for speeding.

In 1946, at the tender age of 19, I effectively saw the end of my brief cycle-racing career. I was working down the mines in very cramped positions during the terribly cold January and February of 1947, which was one of the coldest spells on record. It meant that I suffered from atrophy of the muscles of my lower back and had disc problems, which necessitated my having my spine encased in plaster for three months, and then wearing a surgical support for many years afterwards. Still, the cycle racing was great fun while it lasted and I was always to keep a racing cycle close to hand for the rest of my life.

5

Hilton Main Colliery

Needless to say, the change from working in a cycle shop to working down a pit could not have been more extreme. While I relished the chance to try something different, I had reservations, deep down, about how I would cope with working in narrow tunnels and under low roofs, as much as 2,000 or even 3,000ft below the ground.

For the first week or two we were all despatched to a small training colliery at Longton, near Stoke-on-Trent. I recall that the days were not too bad and, obviously, very instructive. When the training period had been completed satisfactorily we were allocated to a mine where workers were needed, as near as possible to where we lived. In my case it was Hilton Main Colliery on the Cannock Road, about 3 or 4 miles out of Wolverhampton. I was due to start the following Monday morning. To get miners to the site, there was a bus that started from a public house car park near the Danilo Cinema, Brierley Hill, picking up miners along the way through Harts Hill, Dudley, Upper Gornal, Sedgley and Wolverhampton. It started at the unearthly hour of 5.15 a.m. to 5.30 a.m., so I had to completely change my sleeping habits and try to get to bed early.

You had to have arrived at the pit, changed, walked up to the pit-head and collected your lamp before the klaxon sounded at 7 a.m. Seconds late, and you would have had it, because the shutters descended and only men who had their lamps were allowed down the pit on the next cage. After that the cage was needed to draw coal, so it focused the mind somewhat, because there was no transport waiting to take you back home. In order to get back to Brierley Hill you would have to catch three different buses; and of course there would be no pay either. All this after having got out of bed at 4.30 in the morning.

The man in charge of all the surface workers was known as the 'bank manager'. I had to fall in before him along with all the other new recruits that week (one dressed in an off-white riding mackintosh that was very fashionable in those days, but not very practical for working down a pit). The bank manager explained all the procedures for surface work, saying that we would have two weeks' experience there before actually working down the mine.

I somehow got into a team with four hefty miners; we had to walk up the adjacent railway line to trucks full of large steel ring girders for supporting the pit roof that had to be unloaded and stacked. The girders were about 10ft long, being straight for about 6ft, then having a gentle curve. By standing two girders opposite each other on each side of the pit wall they would meet in the middle, where a strong metal coupling plate would be bolted through to fasten them together. Two of our team would climb into the truck and start throwing out the girders (which must have weighed 2cwt each) as though they were playthings. The other three of us waited for them to land so that we could carry them a few yards away and stack them. As they were an unusual shape you had to be careful not to be too near when they landed, for they could bounce in different directions. I soon established myself to lift in the middle of my two hefty workmates, who made light work between them of lifting each end. It did not require much more than 'OK boys, lift now', and we were ready to stack. I quite relished the job.

The two weeks allowed on the surface soon passed. All my friends who had started with me had already been sent down the pit; however, my team of regular surface workers seemed to have taken to me. As I was mentioned in the cycle-racing results in the *Express & Star*, that too went in my favour. They did not want me to go down the pit any more than I did; as it seemed a rather loose arrangement that I would be told to go down when the bank manager saw me, my team went to endless lengths to keep me out of his sight. I actually spent about three months of a very nice summer working with these chunky guys before I was eventually 'sussed out'.

Surprisingly enough to me, the bank manager did not make any big deal of it, but as he was very short of workers on the night shift he did ask me if I would like to have a go at that for a while instead of going down the mine. I thought it might be worth a try, so the next week I set off on my bike at about 8.30 p.m., ready to be on duty for the 10 p.m. surface shift. When I reported I was told that I would be working on 'the screens', which was where the coal was sorted from the 'bats' (stone) and then graded by size onto different conveyor belts. It does not sound too bad, but the working conditions were pretty horrific. First, you were working quite high up in the air because the coal was loaded onto railway wagons that passed underneath the screens. Secondly, the coal was initially moved along by a shaking movement of the large metal conveyors, which created a horrendous noise so that you could only speak to someone by cupping your hands together and shouting right into his ear. Finally, the continuous movement of tons of coal created a tremendous dust which got into your throat and up your nose, even onto your food as you unwrapped it – in fact, everywhere!

The summer months had finished; it was bitterly cold and windy in this somewhat decrepit corrugated-iron structure some 15ft or so in the air – particularly at 2 and 3 a.m! I was courting my first wife, Lorraine, at the time and I missed almost as many shifts as I completed. I found it increasingly difficult to drag myself to such a workplace in the middle of the evening. After a couple of months or so I had to 'bite the bullet' and reconcile myself to going down the pit.

The following Monday I was up at the pub car park at 5.15 a.m., helping the driver to 'crank' the engine of the old pre-war bus, a task with which I would become very familiar because I was the only miner to be picked up at Brierley Hill. I was soon at the colliery, having fallen asleep again before I had gone the mile or so to the first stop at Harts Hill. I awoke roughly 50 minutes later, when the bus took the sharp right turn off the Cannock Road and into the colliery. I was soon sorted out with my lamp and ready at the pit-head, waiting my turn to walk into the cage for the descent. The cage was quite large and held a fair number of miners. It took quite a long time to get down to the pit bottom. The winding gear started slowly, building up speed to 70ft per second before slowing down again to come to a fairly gentle halt at the bottom.

I had no idea where I would be working or what I would be doing, but was informed that I would be working in the pit bottom, which I thought was great because it was quite spacious there, with the high ceilings. It turned out to be not quite that nice because there were three decks on the runways that built up to the cage. I was to be on the middle deck, which was only about 4½ft high, just high enough to allow for the passage of the pit tubs. I had to pull these off the cage as they came back down to the pit empty, ready to send out to the coalface for refilling.

Another thing I very soon found out was that the pit had to have two shafts, one for the passage of coal, pit props, miners and so on, the other to draw fresh air through the workings. I had only been working down the pit for a few weeks before the notorious winter of 1947. This was the worst winter we had had to endure in living memory, with exceptionally low temperatures and a frost that lasted for six weeks. Working right in the pit bottom meant being in an icy blast of air that was being continuously pumped through. The trucks, which had been on the surface for several hours, were icy cold to handle, and difficult to pull off the cage because the grease on the wheel axles had solidified under the extreme weather conditions.

That was the bad news of January and February 1947. The good news was that the mines were nationalised on 1 January and the National Coal Board was formed to run the collieries. The good news from my point of view was that a man had been appointed specifically to liaise with the Bevin Boys. I think one of his priorities was to try to encourage the boys to stay on in the mine after the expiration of their compulsory time. He approached me one day and talked about me staying on and studying for a higher post, possibly to try eventually for a manager's certificate. I listened patiently and told him of my past work experience, including my accountancy. I felt somewhat sorry for him really, because he was a nice, kindly man and I do not think any of the other Bevin Boys had the slightest interest in listening to him – they had not the remotest intention of staying on in the mines. I was a little surprised when, a week or two later, he came creeping along the middle deck to see me again. 'I've just found out that there's a vacancy for a clerk in the accounts office, Geoff,' he said, 'I wondered if you'd like to pop in and see the chief clerk when you finish your shift.'

Would I? You bet I would! After an ultra-quick shower, I made myself as tidy as possible to go along to see Mr Wesley Hinks, the chief clerk. He was a lovely guy and we got on like a house on fire; furthermore, I was appointed on the spot.

The following Monday morning, I was cycling over to Hilton Main to start what was to be a very enjoyable twelve months or so in the accounts office. I got on very well with the staff there and Wesley himself was quite a character. He would often arrive at the office at 9 a.m., fling the door open wide, strike a pose and say,

Days and moments quickly flying, blend the living with the dead.
Soon will you and I be lying, each within his narrow bed!

This was more than fifty years ago. It is strange how you remember some things as though they were yesterday. After a while Wesley promoted me to be his personal assistant, and my job was to help him with his copious workload. One of the things I took over and thoroughly enjoyed was the large and very busy works canteen. I did not do any cooking, but was responsible for all the staff who worked there, also for ordering and sourcing all the foodstuffs and equipment that were required to keep it ticking over on a daily basis.

This experience was to stand me in good stead when my allotted time as a Bevin Boy had been completed. I was ready for a new challenge in life and I thought this was quite possibly a line that I might explore.

6

Pattison Hughes Catering Company

As luck would have it, on my nightly scouring of the *Express & Star* situations vacant column, I read that a canteen manager was required at the large engineering works, Chillington Tool, Willenhall Road, Wolverhampton. I applied for this job and was interviewed by an attractive young lady, who, when I told her of my work experience to date, said, 'I think that with your experience you might be able to handle my job and I will put your name forward for an interview if you like, because I'm leaving shortly.'

She explained her job was with a large catering organisation, Pattison Hughes of Birmingham, and her job was to supervise ten industrial works canteens across the Black Country area. Not long after being interviewed by the management of Pattison Hughes, I was given the job, with the proviso that I underwent a six-week crash course in cooking and canteen management at a canteen in Bearwood, Birmingham.

I was delighted to land such a responsible position at my young age (I was barely 21 at the time) and, with a little trepidation regarding the job I had talked myself into, I caught the bus to Bearwood the following Monday morning. My initial fears were soon dispelled, for the manageress was a kind but efficient and capable person who soon took me under her wing. It was the run-up to Christmas; I was soon indoctrinated into the trussing and cooking of turkeys, then into slicing them and serving with sage and onion stuffing, plus the trimmings. To give you some idea of the costings for this, the standard charge for a two-course meal was 1*s*, and Pattison Hughes had to make their profit out of that.

The six weeks soon passed and had been an excellent grounding for when I took over the ten canteens spread across Wolverhampton and the Black Country. My job was to see that all the canteens ran as efficiently as possible; in the event of a chef or manageress not being able to turn up for work at short notice, I would have to take over the role. It was quite a task to keep constantly in close contact with all ten canteens. I soon found out, however, that one or two of the smaller ones were well run and did not require regular monitoring; therefore, I could concentrate on the larger canteens, one of which had to produce 500 meals per day.

When I had been in the post a few months my boss, the man in charge of all the canteen supervisors, approached me one day to say, 'I have a wonderful opportunity

Brierley Hill High Street in the 1950s, showing the Town Hall with public clock, where we used to go dancing.

for you at Castle Bromwich soon, Geoff. The British Industries Fair is being staged there and we are doing the catering for it and I would like you to run a large bar and buffet there.'

The British Industries Fair, or the BIF as it became known, was staged in 1949 to try to kick-start British industry, which had taken a pounding during the war years. Potential buyers from all over the world were invited to visit the stands of British manufacturers, to start re-creating the trading conditions which had prevailed in pre-war times.

A week or two later I was catching the first bus from Brierley Hill at some unearthly hour, then changing at Birmingham to get another bus out to Castle Bromwich, where I was to report as soon as possible after 7 a.m. I eventually arrived and found the Pattison Hughes office, joining a long queue of thirty-two other people waiting for it to open. When it did all the ladies in front of me handed in their appropriate paperwork; then I who was last, handed in mine. 'Oh, you're Mr Hill,' the lady exclaimed. 'All these ladies are your staff and these are your keys for C2 bar and buffet. As soon as you get there you'll find a requisition list. Please complete it straight away and phone it through to our central stores. The doors are open to the public at 9 a.m.; you'll need all your drinks and food ready for then, so you haven't got much time.'

You can say that again! I walked quickly through the giant, aircraft-hangar-like halls, with my entourage of ladies of all ages, until I found C2. Opening it up, I went to work straight away, ordering up supplies by telephone from the long list. It transpired that Pattison Hughes did catering for functions at various county cricket matches, horse races, weddings etc., so my band of women was very experienced. Quite soon, they had all sorted themselves out as to who was going to work in the bar, who would serve on the buffet and who would be preparing the food, doing washing up, etc. It soon started to fit into place and, as the exhibition centre began to fill up, we became very busy. Business peaked just after lunch each day, when we had a small stock of cigarettes and tobacco, which were still in very short supply. After a day or two the word got around and we had an enormous queue of people waiting to get their hands on a few Woodbines or Players.

The exhibition lasted about eleven days and on the day it finished the two managing directors asked me to come to their office. I went along and was invited to sit down. One of them said, 'I don't know how you've managed to do it, Mr Hill. In fact, I don't know whether we want to know.'

It transpired that everything I had ordered from the stores had been broken down into the retail price that it would generate: so many shots out of a bottle of whisky, etc., then they were all added together and a comparison made with the total takings raised on that day. It appeared that in my case I had raised more cash than had been expected on every day! They were both delighted and complimentary, awarding me a sizeable bonus in my next wage packet. Later I found that the bar staff, who also did all the race meetings and other functions, were giving slightly short measures on drinks, and this had added up to quite a surplus over the whole exhibition. It was only when they confided in me that I realised they might well have been helping themselves to a copper or two as well.

While working at Castle Bromwich, I made friends with the manager of the Spa Hotel, Buxton; before the exhibition finished he had invited me to join him there as assistant manager. It was a very tempting offer but I was shortly to be married and I knew my wife would not relish a complete change of environment. In any case, I had by then already made arrangements for us to live in one half of The Gables. However, even today I sometimes reflect on how my life would have changed if I had accepted this offer, at one of the many crossroads in my life.

The time I spent with Pattison Hughes had been most interesting and certainly quite a challenge at my age, but after eighteen months or so things were beginning to become a little routine and I started to get 'itchy feet' for a new challenge in life.

7

A Travelling Salesman

I had thought for some time that I would like to try and find a post as a travelling salesman and most evenings looked through the situations vacant column in the *Express & Star*.

I soon found out that I was still quite young to be a sales representative, and although I grew a moustache to make myself look older, I was lacking in any sales experience to land a job with a reputable organisation. I realised, however, that it was quite possible to be a door-to-door salesman and be paid a on 'commission only' basis on sales, so I decided to get my foot on the bottom rung of the ladder, signing up with Kleen-e-ze to sell brushes and polish in the Halesowen area.

I remember it was quite daunting at first, as hardly anyone went round door-to-door selling in those days; however, I soon developed the technique of having a duster ready in my hand with some Kleen-e-ze polish on it. As the lady came to the door, I would rub it on a small circle of the dirty door-frame, so that when I polished it a few seconds later it shone as if it was brand new. Many of the homes were terraced houses that hadn't seen a lick of paint for ten years or more and it was as if I had performed some magic trick. It was then reasonably easy to complete a sale of a large tin of polish, and occasionally one of the brushes as well.

It so happened that my grandfather, who was a retired wholesale and retail fruit and vegetable trader in Old Hill, lived within the area I was canvassing. One day I knocked on his door – much to his surprise and consternation. I had what I thought was a reasonable chat with him about what I was doing, but later was to hear from his son, my uncle, that Geoffrey had called round 'begging'. I don't think he altogether agreed with what, to him, was a new way of trading.

I made reasonable money with Kleen-e-ze during the few months I was with them, but it was no fun when the weather deteriorated; so I was still constantly scanning the situations vacant columns and writing off to any sales vacancy that I thought appropriate.

One of these was with Encyclopaedia Britannica, which produced and published its many-volume bound books of endless knowledge on a whole variety of topics. These were sold direct to the householder or institute, but instead of direct canvassing, many of the sales were made by following up leads generated from their advertisements. After the usual week or so of training I was on my own, once again selling on a 'commission only' basis, but this time the sales were destined to take an hour or more to complete. The volumes were only sold as a complete set. With full leather binding, I remember them as costing something in the region of £200, a tremendous amount of money in those days. They also published a cheaper version with leather quarter-bindings, and at the bottom of the range a hard-bound cloth-covered variety, which was sold at about £80 – still quite a lot of money. Most of the sales were made to parents with children still at school and were made on the basis that they would always have at their disposal this wonderful fountain of knowledge to further their education, so enabling them to really make something of their lives. As very few parents had this kind of money, practically all of the sales were made on hire-purchase, with the balance paid in monthly instalments over two or three years.

Another very unwelcome obstacle put in the representatives' way was that they were only allowed to sell a certain percentage of the cheaper, cloth-bound version; at least one in three sales had to be of the upmarket, leather-bound or quarter-bound variety. This was the part I didn't warm to. It was bad enough to me to load a person with a few years of paying back the instalments for books which, in the underprivileged area of the Black Country, would in all likelihood never be used anything like as much as they were intended to be. I found leaving them with twice the amount of debt for just a better binding difficult to handle, but I was in trouble if I didn't accede to it.

After a few weeks I received an enquiry from Malvern College, which was quite a way to drive in my old 1927 Austin 10. I reported there dressed in my Sunday best, asking to speak to the gentleman that had initiated the enquiry, presumably one of the teachers. Some 15 minutes later the receptionist returned looking rather puzzled, stating that unfortunately there was no one of that name employed on their payroll: had I somehow got it wrong? On further investigation I noticed that it did not say 'Mr' before the name, so I suggested that perhaps it was one of the mature students who had initiated the enquiry. The receptionist went off again to investigate the student register, eventually returning with a very sheepish-looking 13-year-old who apologised for having caused me to drive all the way to Malvern, adding that he had thought they would just send some details through the post. The pupils there were residents from all over the country, so there was no way I could follow up the enquiry with his parents. So I had a look around Malvern before disconsolately wending my way home.

After a few months I became increasingly disillusioned with the job, particularly having to sell an expensive product, which, good as it undoubtedly was, would, in my opinion, never be used extensively by the family. I was loading up two or three years' debt for books that would end up collecting dust on shelves in the spare room. I thought I might do better to go back to my office work for a while until the right selling job came along.

Quite soon afterwards I had an interview and was accepted for a job in the accounts department of Tube Investments, a very large firm in Oldbury. It was the first time that I had worked in a large office block and I never settled enough to say that I enjoyed the job. As the new boy on the block, part of my duties was to take the post and other documents round to the various offices. I suppose that although I was still quite young I had already managed to hold down much more responsible jobs. I'm sure that if I had worked at it long enough there could have been promotion prospects, but early indications were that it would be a long way down the line. My patience finally ran out after just a few weeks, when I could see that this job was just not for me, so I told the boss and left immediately.

I was still having occasional interviews for a sales representative or accounting work. After a few days I was successful in finding a job in control of invoicing and accounts at a small engineering works called the Dudley Non-Ferrous Castings Company, at Dudley. I was to start there on the Monday morning of the following week. I immediately liked the set-up because the owner was an engineer who had built up the business himself. Although he knew a great deal about engineering, he knew little about accounts and needed someone to take care of that side of his business. I was to be in total control of the office and had three nice, friendly young ladies to do letters and invoices. It seemed my sort of job.

I was amazed when I opened my morning mail a couple of days later, to receive notification of an interview for the post of sales representative at Glovers Typewriters, in Darlington Street, Wolverhampton. To cap it all, the interview was at 5 p.m, on the Monday that I was to start my new job. Enticing as the prospects seemed at my new office job, deep down I still relished the idea of being an outdoor sales representative, and I could in no way forgo this opportunity to see if I had the potential to land such a job.

The Monday morning came and I presented myself at Dudley for my new office manager role, immediately explaining to the boss that unfortunately I had a prior arrangement requiring me to leave at 4 p.m. that day, and hoping that it would be permissible. He in turn was quite understanding, so at 4 in the afternoon I was on my way to Wolverhampton to find Glovers Typewriters and present myself for my interview. It was not at all as daunting as I had expected or had experienced in selling interviews over the preceding years. The founder, Mr Glover, had built up the business, but had died some years previously. His widow, who still helped in the showroom, and her son, a very quiet and somewhat introverted man who was trying with difficulty to fill his father's shoes, were interviewing me. The firm had built up contacts with a great number of the many engineering and manufacturing businesses in the Wolverhampton, Bilston and Willenhall areas. It was to be my job to develop these, and at the same time to canvass other firms in the locality, in an effort to expand the business. My previous selling experience with Kleen-e-ze and Encyclopaedia Britannica stood me in good stead even though both had been commission-only paying jobs. They seemed to like the look of me and the wage was agreeable, and they wanted to know when I could start. Oh dear! I tried to say in a matter-of-fact way that I would probably have to give my current employer two weeks' notice, and if that was so, then I would telephone them the next day.

Suddenly, I was in a quandary. I had quite enjoyed my few hours working in the Dudley office and I am certain I could have settled down there for a few years if this other opportunity had not presented itself. I was to find in later life that I was only completely happy when I was left to work for myself – or at least unsupervised; this job certainly seemed to fill those criteria. By the time I arrived for work the next day I had definitely decided that it was to be the selling job for me, so I had the unenviable task of explaining the whole situation to my employer of one day and asking if I could, regrettably, terminate my employment. Once he had recovered from the initial shock he was quite understanding, asking me only if I would mind working two weeks' notice so that the office work didn't get in arrears while he was advertising for a new manager. Of course I agreed to do this, and later in the day phoned Glovers, explaining that I had submitted my notice and would commence in two weeks' time. Looking back on those two weeks I can only remember them as days when I was enjoying every minute of being left in total control in a small office, having lovely young ladies making cups of tea or coffee, and also bringing me back cakes on their odd shopping expeditions. All the time I was wondering if I was doing the right thing in forgoing all these niceties to go out into the cold world of canvassing for new customers. However, I had made my decision, and much as I regretted leaving it all behind on my last day, I was up and ready for the challenge by the next Monday morning.

I soon found Mrs Glover and her son to be lovely people and very kind, but certainly not the business persons that Mr Glover must have been. When I came in with my orders at the end of each day there would be more enthusiasm shown for a large order of typing paper, typewriter ribbons, pencils or box files than for one for a couple of typewriters, which would come to many times the value of the office stationery orders. When I had been there a few months Olivetti, the Italian typewriter manufacturer, released the first electric typewriter. I went mad taking the demonstration model round to all our customers and collecting orders for this 'must have' item! When they arrived at Glovers a month or two later, I remember them being quite troublesome and prone to break down, as most new electrical items were in those days. It was probably after being there about six months that my enthusiasm for the job started to decline a little, especially if I was having a poor sales day and the weather was bad. I would lose interest in the job, spending an hour or two in the reading room of a local library, or part of the afternoon in a cinema until it was time to report back to the Glovers showroom with whatever orders I had taken, before going home. I mention all this because, one afternoon, I had dived out of the pouring rain and into a cinema in Wolverhampton, sitting in the middle section on the back row. It was a good thing that I had not sat a couple of rows further forward, because, as the lights went up in the interval, I saw sitting immediately in front of me none other than my employer, the young Mr Glover! I immediately moved out into the aisle, and was about to sidle out of the cinema, when I thought, 'What the hell, why waste my cinema ticket?' So I crept along the back row and sat right up in the corner for practically the whole of the film, sneaking out just before the lights went up. I don't think Mr Glover was a very good salesman and I guess that he didn't enjoy it any more than I did when he was having a bad day!

It was not long after this episode that I made contact with a Mr Baker, of Baker's Typewriters, Walsall. This was a totally different set-up, as the business was quite new, having been started by Mr Baker only a few years earlier. He was a very go-ahead businessman and immediately wanted me to go and work for his company, but still largely covering the same sales territory as Glovers. The extra cash he offered me was too big to refuse, so, after trying to explain as kindly as I could to the Glover family, I handed in my notice and was soon setting off for Walsall each day. Although Baker's was a much more organised and ambitious firm to work for, my early enthusiasm soon started to wane, and it was back to the situations vacant column with a vengeance.

8

A Hoover Sales/Service Representative

I was beginning to realise that being a sales representative and calling on firms was not exactly what I was looking for. If things were not going well on the sales front it was very discouraging and the days seemed very long and lonely. I saw a post advertised for a sales/service representative in the local area with Hoover, paying a small basic wage for the twenty-one service overhauls that had to be completed in customers' houses every week; also a quite handy commission on all sales, including those made by your dealer.

I had my interview and was accepted. Very soon I was off to Manchester and staying in lodgings for a few weeks, to go through the very comprehensive courses in selling and servicing Hoover cleaners. Not being a particularly mechanically minded person I found the service courses very educational. But when it came to the selling course I found it very basic and quite boring, as I had by now spent some considerable time out on the road selling for four different companies. The Hoover sales technique was all from a prepared text, designed mainly for men with no previous selling experience, as was the case with most of those on my course. They included bus drivers, factory workers, painters and decorators etc., and all benefited from having precise words put in their mouths. But when I had to stand in front of the class I always used my own interpretation of the sales patter to complete the sale, much to the annoyance of the instructor, who would invariably stop me in full flight and say, 'Oh no, not like that, Mr Hill', going on to explain the 'Hoover way' to sell a product. We built up a love/hate relationship throughout the remainder of the course.

Our paths were to cross some years later, when I was out with my Stourbridge supervisor and had to collect our new manager for the Walsall branch, of which I was part. After a brief introduction I sat in the back seat of the car while the new manager sat in the front with my supervisor, Bill Hindmarsh. Expecting to surprise the manager, I started by saying, 'I actually know you, sir. You taught me at Manchester when I was on my Hoover training course.'

His reply surprised me because he must have taught many hundreds of new recruits over the years. 'I certainly remember you, Mr Hill,' he said. 'I remember you very well indeed.' I detected from his tone that I had made a lasting impression on him, and from then on we both got on exceedingly well.

After I passed the Hoover course I was allocated part of Stourbridge as my territory for sales and service, and was also told that my dealer would be Pargeters, the furniture store in Stourbridge. Each representative had a dealer allocated to him. He was then required to follow up any possible business enquiries generated by the dealer, receiving commission on all sales made. It was therefore a very important part of my ongoing earning potential and I couldn't wait to be introduced there. At 9 a.m. on the Monday I met the Hoover supervisor at a café in Stourbridge; half an hour later he took me round to the furniture store to meet Mr Pargeter. We made our way through the store, into his office and I was introduced to the rather dour-looking Mr Pargeter, who opened the conversation by saying, 'I want you to know, Mr Hill, that we don't give any cash discounts, we don't do any hire-purchase and we don't take any part exchanges.'

My heart sank instantly. At a stroke I had been deprived of all the financial negotiating that usually encompassed a sale. I'm afraid that I came out of the showroom a far less happy man than when I had entered it some 5 minutes earlier.

As things turned out it was not all bad news, for I eventually found other dealers who were quite flexible on payments and part exchanges, and keen to accept any sales that I could generate. I eventually struck up quite a rapport with a Mr William Williams of Bridgnorth, who had built up a wonderful, small department store business in High Town. After a while he was not only letting me negotiate my own deals on sales, but also giving me an extra cash incentive as well.

At last I seemed to have found a job that fulfilled most of my requirements. As there were twenty-one service overhauls to complete in the home, I had every incentive to be out on the job early each morning. It was while I was doing the servicing that I was able to talk to the customer with a view to updating her old (usually pre-war) Hoover vacuum cleaner. If she already had a modern one I would be enquiring if she knew of any neighbours or relatives who might be interested in having a free demonstration. This type of selling worked remarkably well because, invariably, after I had cleaned a carpet or two, emptied the dustbag onto a piece of newspaper and confronted the person with a quite large pile of dust and dirt, completing the sale was just a formality. However, I found that there was an even better chance of completing the sale in the evening, when the husband was present. Therefore, I often left the cleaner in the daytime for the housewife to use, returning that evening to conclude the sale.

There was little need for cold canvassing, but occasionally we would have to have a purge in a new area that wasn't covered by our sales/service team. One of these was arranged at Kinlet, a small mining village the far side of the Severn, near Bridgnorth. Hoover had just brought out a new, spherical, suction cleaner called the Hoover Constellation, so I thought I would try this one out for a change. My patter went something like this:

'Good morning, Madam, I'm from Hoover Limited and we are just doing a market research on a brand new cleaner and would be obliged if you would try it out in your home for us; just to give us your candid opinion of it. We are not selling the cleaner; we just want to know what you think of it.'

The few cleaners I had, I soon managed to get placed in the same row of small, miners' cottages. Twenty-four hours later I repeated the quite long journey back to Kinlet and was knocking on the door of the first cottage. When the door was opened I was disappointed to see that the Constellation had been repackaged and was waiting at the lady's feet, so I said, 'Oh, I'm surprised to see that you've packed it all away, I thought you would be so pleased with it that you'd still be using it.' Her reply knocked me sideways. 'Oh, your cleaner was brilliant,' she said, 'but you did say that you were not selling yours and there happened to be a man round from Vactrix in the afternoon and he was selling his, so I bought one!'

Vactrix was our main competitor in those days and I felt a right fool to have made this sale so easy for them. To make matters worse I don't think any of the other cleaners I had left resulted in sales either. The cottages were very small and, as black and white television had recently come onto the market, it was the only electrical appliance that most were interested in buying! I stayed with Hoover for some four and a half years, much longer than any of my previous jobs, and had many humorous incidents during that time. Just one of these I'll recount now, although it wasn't funny at the time.

It was a Friday afternoon and I was struggling to complete the last of my twenty-one service overhauls, calling at a corner shop in Kidderminster that I had been to before on six-monthly check-ups. The lady who owned the shop was very busy with weekend shoppers and asked would I mind leaving it over until the next week: I agreed to this. As it was getting towards the end of my time at Hoover, I had condensed everything down from a large metal box to the barest minimum of tools, belts and brushes, which I carried in a black leather briefcase. By then I had also bought a new, black Austin A30 car, so I looked quite smart for a service engineer. The following Monday, at 9 a.m. sharp, I knocked at the front door of the residential part of the shop. The lady let me in and immediately went up the stairs. 'Up here,' she cried hurriedly. 'Up there?' I replied. I climbed the stairs thinking it somewhat unusual, as most people wanted the vacuum cleaners serviced in the kitchen or on sheets of newspaper in the sitting room. She then walked quickly along the landing and into one of the bedrooms, saying, 'In here, please.' I swiftly responded by entering the bedroom, and was astonished to see an elderly gentleman propped up in the bed, looking very pale, with blood trickling from the corners of his mouth. 'Good gracious,' I exclaimed, 'what on earth has happened?' 'He's had a haemorrhage, as I explained on the phone,' she hastily replied. Seeing that I was still rooted to the spot, she added, 'You are the doctor, aren't you?' 'No,' I stuttered, 'I'm your Hoover representative. I've come to service the Hoover!'

As I said, it was not funny at the time, but I have had a few laughs over the years in recounting this little tale. A few days later, when the elderly gentleman had fully recovered, we were both able to laugh about it. The lady knew they had a new locum working at the doctor's practice and presumed I was he, when I turned up a few minutes after she had phoned. She said that I looked more like a doctor than a service engineer!

Hoover introduced their first hand-wringer washing machine during my years with them. It only held 3½lb of clothes and had to be emptied through a rubber tube into a drain or by bucket. Like Hoover cleaners, the washing machines had to be demonstrated in the home in those days, because people had never seen one working before. Everyone washed on a Monday morning then, so I was often out with washing machines in the different houses at 9, 10 and 11 a.m. Once there, I demonstrated the washer by loading it with hot water (the first washers had no heaters), adding soap powder and loading the first of the clothes for a 4-minute wash. I then put the clothes through the wringer and showed how to empty the machine. I then let the lady carry on with her washing while I moved to the next appointment.

I remember one occasion when I had just moved my territory to cover the centre of Kidderminster and had talked myself into giving a washing machine demonstration in a very old pub there. I arrived early one Monday morning and the landlady had told me that she always did her washing in the bathroom, which was, naturally, located upstairs. I struggled with the washer up two flights of stairs and into the bathroom, then slowly filled it up with hot water from a little water heater over the sink. Putting the washing and soap powder in, I found a decrepit old socket by the door, put the plug in and switched on. Nothing happened! Suddenly, an irate voice shouted from below, 'I suppose you know we're on DC here? You've blown the bloody fuses!' 'No, I'm afraid I didn't know,' I replied.

DC or direct current was a totally different electrical supply to the alternating current in general use today. You can imagine that I was not the most popular boy in town, having to empty the washer, leave all the washing and get out of the place as quickly as possible. Actually, I was very unlucky, for it was only a very small part of old Kidderminster town that was still waiting to be converted from DC to AC.

Hoover had lots of sales competitions and I had to compete with the other sixty or so other representatives based in the Walsall district. The main ones of the year were the Christmas Competition and the Derby Contest. For these, which usually ran for six to eight weeks, a weekly points sheet was distributed so that you knew exactly where you stood at any time during the contest. During the last few weeks it became really frantic, and you never quite knew what you were up against. The commissions you earned were paid on each guarantee card submitted. However, some representatives held cards back, only to push them through all together in the very last week! I did manage to win the Christmas Competition a couple of times, which meant that I was awarded an enormous Christmas hamper as well as all the additional commission earned from the many extra sales I had generated over the period.

The highlight of the year, however, was the Hoover Derby Contest, when the winner and his wife were invited to stay at the Strand Palace Hotel, London, and also had seats on an open-top double-decker bus near the finishing line of the Derby on Epsom Downs. Among the other entertainment laid on was a Grand Ball at Hoover's wonderful headquarters at Perivale, near the London inner ring road. The last full year that I worked for Hoover I managed to win the 'big one', and I remember it as being quite an occasion in the 1950s for my wife and me to see all the wonderful London sights for the first time. I also remember it because about ten months later, just before I handed in my notice, I was at the district meeting at Walsall. Here, details of the following year's Derby Contest were being spelled out to the sixty-odd representatives, all dressed in their best suits and assembled before the district and Midland regional managers, who were also there for this special occasion. I had lost a lot of interest in the job, for reasons that I'll describe shortly, and had not bothered to change; I was in my old working jacket and was sitting at the back of the hall. Imagine my surprise at being called during the interval, because the district and regional managers wanted to speak to me. I immediately dashed to the toilet to straighten my tie, comb my hair and generally try to smarten myself up. I mounted the stage at the end of the room where the two managers were sitting behind a table. 'Oh, there you are, Mr Hill,' the district manager exclaimed, quickly introducing me to our regional manager. 'We were getting worried that you weren't present at the meeting. What we'd like you to do is to address the Walsall representatives for 10 to 15 minutes to tell them all about your recollections of winning the Derby Contest last year.'

I was completely taken aback as I had never done any public speaking before and hardly looked dressed for the part. However, there were many lovely experiences to recount of a young man from the Black Country being in the 'big city' for the first time. I managed to raise a few laughs and the quarter of an hour passed all too quickly.

9

Severnside Stores

While I was still with Hoover, my girlfriend Lorraine Jackson and I decided to get married at 'Top Church' (as it was known in Dudley). It was 1949 and I was just 22 years old when we tied the knot, then settling down together in the part of The Gables that I had been living in for some years.

I was usually able to make plenty of sales with my Hoover job and it was paying quite good money; also, it was always rewarding to me to know that I was selling a product that was very useful and efficient. When I called in a week or two later to see how they were getting on with it, many customers would thank me quite sincerely for selling it to them: at the same time I would ask if any of their friends were in the market for one.

Geoff's Severnside Stores at Bewdley was the white building in the left of the picture. It had a beautiful view of the River Severn.

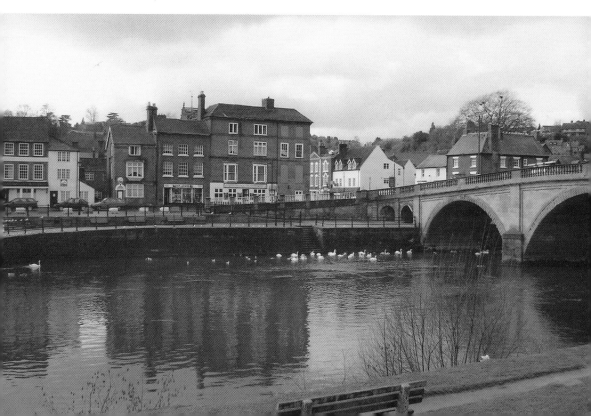

I had some savings in the bank and started seriously looking for a business, preferably with living accommodation, which Lorraine could run. After nearly clinching a deal (which fell through at the last minute) for a little corner grocery shop at Willenhall, I came across a shop in a beautiful location by the river at Bewdley, quite close to the attractive old bridge. A young lady in her mid-twenties had been running it for a few years as a sausage, bacon and cooked-meats shop. Although she had no current accounts to show me, the ones that she had showed quite a good profit, and I knew she had been opening for only a few hours a week so I thought there was a lot of potential here. It was only some time later, after we had moved in, that I found she had done well because she was a close friend of the manager of the large Marsh & Baxter pork butcher's shop in Kidderminster. He had supplied her with ample quantities of their products, many of which had been in very short supply after the war. These were the account years that the crafty young lady had chosen to show me to negotiate the sale.

However, all was not lost, and although the shop was quite tiny I proceeded to turn it into a fully-fledged grocery store, creating a display of fruit and vegetables in the area just outside the shop. The non-existent living accommodation upstairs had been used for mixing and making lead paint, which was inches thick around the walls and became a maze of colours when chipped off.

As the paint was removed, the old plaster came away too, so the whole room had to be replastered and a new brick fireplace built in. The far end of the room was curtained off to make our bedroom, and had a beautiful view overlooking the Severn, with the swans gliding down under the bridge only a few yards away. Closer inspection of the window revealed names and dates scratched onto the panes; the dates went back to the 1870s. As we entered the door to the first floor, there was a tiny space that just about sufficed to make a minute kitchen. The worst part I have kept until last. Upstairs was approached by exiting the shop at the side and climbing what could only be described as a wooden ladder. This had been quite substantially built many years ago, but was now breaking up with dry rot and old age. However, it had to manage for a few more months until we had the cash to have brick and concrete stairs constructed, housing a coal store underneath.

I managed to get my Hoover territory transferred from Stourbridge to Kidderminster, and had an old-established electrical retailer, B. French Ltd, of Mill Street, Kidderminster, as my dealer. They were really involved in electrical installation work in places such as the remoter areas of Scotland, the retail side being a very much smaller part of the organisation.

Working for Hoover tied in well with the shop, as I had no set hours and was able to do odd jobs in the daytime as well as promoting the shop on service calls in and around Bewdley. Lorraine worked hard at building up a regular clientele, but I do remember that we came unstuck with one or two who had their goods on 'tick' during the week, and then never came in with the cash when pay-day came around on Friday.

During the summer months we had a large influx of visitors, mainly by train from Birmingham; we could see them come streaming across the bridge in droves from the station, particularly on Sunday mornings. It was usually then that Lorraine didn't want to open the shop because she'd already done Monday until Saturday. I, on the other hand, could see the opportunity to make good money by selling locally grown cherries, loads of ice cream and sweets, all of which carried a much larger profit margin than groceries.

Talking of ice cream, I had managed to become an agent for Lyons ice cream, which, together with Walls, was the front runner in the ice cream stakes after the war. Deliveries came by rail in those days, in a large insulated container filled with ice cream and dry ice. Our freezer was really quite small and, as it was a three-day delivery on Lyons ice cream, it was a real balancing act to know when to order. If the weather became inclement for the weekend we had no back-up facilities for storing it. I suddenly happened on a solution that worked remarkably well during the remainder of the three years we were there. I found a small manufacturer called Morcream, at Wollaston, Stourbridge, who made long cutting blocks of ice cream that could be cut and sold between two wafers. It was really nice and I would hear customers walking away after having been served, saying how good it was and how they always went for Lyons ice cream! It was also very profitable to sell it this way; a quick journey over to Wollaston, and I could restock my freezer in half an hour or so. Bewdley had lots of cherry orchards quite close to the town and we would sell dozens of baskets of this lovely fruit when in season.

After about three years or so I started getting 'itchy feet' again and began looking in all the newspapers for business opportunities. I remember one weekend persuading Lorraine to drive with me down to Margate on the south-east coast to view a fish-and-chip shop that was for sale and supposed to be doing good business. We couldn't leave Bewdley on the Saturday until we had closed the shop at about 5 p.m., so it was 10 p.m. by the time we arrived in Margate. We found the fish-and-chip shop, which didn't look particularly inspiring. When I talked to the vendor he explained that when you served the chips you squeezed the bottom sides of the bag together, so that although it looked as if you were filling it to the top; in reality the customer was getting a lot less than appeared. Needless to say, we were not excited at the prospect of buying such a place. By the time we left it was after 11 p.m., too late to get accommodation, so we had an uncomfortable few hours' sleep in the car before the long haul back to Bewdley the next day.

It dawned on me that we might have some difficulty selling the shop with its rather unusual living accommodation, so I thought that I had better try to sell it first, then, hopefully, find a suitable business. After a while I found a fairly elderly spinster who thought the shop would suit her fine and, as she was flexible about moving in, I could start looking around in earnest for another place.

10

The Hop Pole Inn

It was 9 a.m. on Monday, the day after finding a buyer for my shop in Bewdley, and I was with the other three representatives who covered the Kidderminster/Stourport/Bewdley area for our usual Monday morning informal meeting. I was telling them that I was looking for a new business somewhere, and to keep their eyes open for me, when one of the reps, Ron Pillinger, said, 'I know where there's a tenancy of a pub for sale at Bewdley. It's called the Hop Pole and it's the one about half a mile up the Cleobury Road on the right hand side.'

Never having been a great frequenter of pubs, I asked him if there was any money to be made from one. 'Oh yes,' he replied. 'When I was young my mother and father had one near Evesham; that's where I was brought up and we always did all right.'

I thought it sounded interesting, so at lunchtime I drove up to the Hop Pole, a black and white inn standing back from the road that, very appropriately, had hops growing over its front entrance. I went inside into a big bar room with a movable wooden partition at the far end. This opened to reveal another room of the same size; ideal for large numbers of people in the summer. Facing the road and not quite as big as the bar, was another nice room called the lounge. Outside, there was a grassed area with seating, also a section with a rain shelter.

I remember ordering half a pint of bitter and feeling a little awkward because I knew so little about pubs. Chatting to the publican, I discovered he was wishing to retire and that I had to contact Marstons Breweries of Burton at their Worcester offices, if I was to take the matter further. I contacted them, and a few days later Lorraine and I went along to be interviewed to see if we would make suitable landlords of the Hop Pole. After an hour or so, I believe we had convinced them that, although totally inexperienced, we had lots of potential, and they agreed to take us on as tenants. Shortly afterwards we moved from the one room that we had managed with over the shop, into the spacious living accommodation at the Hop Pole.

It was a very steep learning curve for the first week or two, finding out how to look after beer, tap and tilt barrels, change them when empty, and clean the pipes weekly, as well as stocking all the other drinks, crisps and snacks. The locals seemed a very friendly bunch, as you would expect them to be. Many worked in the carpet factories in Kidderminster and we were soon to know them all and what they drank. Most would come in at the same time every night, sit in the same seat and drink the same number of pints: real creatures of habit.

The Hop Pole Inn as it is today.

In winter, we had people come with jugs to the 'outdoor' window to have a couple of pints to take back to the council houses situated just across the road. This practice increased because it was the 1950s, when black and white television was just becoming popular, and people were fascinated by this new form of entertainment that they could have in their homes.

As spring arrived everything started to change. There were about 120 caravans in the fields behind the Hop Pole, many owned by small-business people from the Birmingham area. Their owners would start reopening them for weekend breaks in the early spring. On Saturday nights in particular, people would pile into the bar extension area, bringing their tambourines and maracas to accompany the piano that one of them would be playing. They were lovely, fun nights, with lots of singing and people packed in like sardines. What amazed me was that odd locals, who would normally drive around in winter having just one drink in several pubs, would stay at the Hop Pole all night, even though they had to stand, while their beer was getting spilled over the quarry-tiled floor from all the jostling!

Birds have always fascinated me, and I read in *Exchange & Mart* that a macaw was for sale at a place on the coast of East Anglia. I arranged to go and see it, leaving at dawn for the long drive in my little Austin A30 car. When I arrived and saw this beautiful red, blue and green macaw I immediately struck a deal, bringing him back next to me in his cage and talking to him most of the way. Mac, as we called him, was an instant attraction in the pub and we soon built up a close bond. I could do anything with Mac, including have him disappear head-first down inside my jumper! He seemed to love to make people laugh and would join in heartily with them. One of his tricks was to have a spoonful of beer, drink it very gracefully and then bend the spoon in his beak. His mandibles were remarkably strong. Another party piece was to get about ten of the large old pennies from the till into his beak, clamber over to the customer's side of the bar and drop them 3 or 4ft onto the red quarry-tiled floor below, where they would bang and scatter. Everybody thought this was quite hilarious and Mac would join in the hearty laughter, sometimes rough and loud, other times quite refined, mimicking the different sounds he was hearing. He was very jealous of me and disliked the large, smoke-grey cat that I had, which would sometimes jump onto my lap seeking affection. Mac would chase him off in seconds!

Food was no big deal in pubs in those days, but to supplement the usual bag of crisps Lorraine cooked a large leg of pork on Saturday nights, which I carved for sandwiches. In the early days we had a few cycling clubs visit for Sunday afternoon tea; but Lorraine was not very keen, so we soon finished that element of the trade.

After a while I started to lose interest in combining working for Hoover together with running the Hop Pole, particularly in the summertime, when we were extremely busy with visitors. So I decided to leave Hoover and look around for something else, preferably self-employed, so that I could control the hours that I worked. One day I spotted in a Birmingham newspaper that the father was retiring from a father-and-son racecourse bookmaker's business and the son was looking for a new partner. I thought, would this be what I had been looking for? We met a few days later and, although I had been to race meetings a few times, I obviously had no experience of bookmaking, but he agreed that we give it a go.

A week or so later was the Cheltenham Gold Cup meeting, held in March each year. On the first morning of the meeting, at 9 a.m., I collected my bookmaker friend from his house in the suburbs of Birmingham. We also had to collect two other men from their homes on the way, one being the man who chalked the prices on the board, the second a tic-tac man who transferred bets into the ring, the inner sanctum at the racecourse.

It was bitterly cold all day, standing at the racecourse, exposed to the biting wind. I remember my two main jobs were to go and get hot cups of Bovril on a regular basis and to have both hands tightly on the large leather bag holding the money – especially when the race was on! Apparently it is then, when everyone is watching the horses racing, that robberies take place, snatching either the whole bag or just a handful of pound notes. We had started the day by putting £100 each into the bag. After the last of the six races, we each took out our original £100 and there seemed quite a nice amount of cash left. It was only after paying out our two helpers, course fees, hot drinks and meals to and from the racecourse, as well as the petrol used, that it brought the winnings down to about £3 each! As I had left the Hop Pole at 8 a.m. and didn't get back till 10 p.m., it didn't inspire me; although I thought tomorrow could be a totally different day.

When the alarm went off at 7 a.m. next day, I'm afraid I just turned over and went back to sleep for an extra hour. My partner rang a little later and I explained that a bookmaker I would never be, although towards the end of my tenure of the Hop Pole I did start to take bets that were passed on to a bookmaker in Kidderminster.

My next enterprise proved to be more enduring. I made contact with another Birmingham man who employed some outworkers making Devon pixies in various poses, all cast in plaster moulds; also, he had a couple of artistic ladies to hand-paint the finished products. He had a very old pre-war furniture van to distribute the goods to the various tourist areas. I made a deal with him, setting off the next Monday morning to collect and pay for all the boxes of pixies awaiting collection. Then, after a journey or two, I would go to Walsall on Monday afternoons to buy leather goods from small manufacturers there, also a few brass items. On Tuesdays I drove as far as Somerset, selling quite a number of items to shops in the Cheddar Gorge. The next day I would drive down to Minehead in Somerset, then on to Lynton and Lynmouth, ending up at Ilfracombe and selling more goods at all these popular seaside places. Thursdays I drove across Dartmoor to Cockington Forge, a well-known tourist attraction near Torquay, where I sold a lot of the brass castings that I had brought with me from Walsall. The tourists all thought they were made in the forge before their very eyes! Usually I stayed the night with a man in Torquay who acted as an agent for me; he eventually built up thirty or forty outlets selling pixies. It is difficult to realise now that there was very little giftware available so soon after the end of the war; the public would buy the simplest things to take home as holiday gifts.

My poor old van was often a source of trouble. It was difficult to start and with very poor brakes, especially on steep hills, and I also had trouble with the radiator leaking, but someone told me that a fresh egg cracked in it would solve the problem. So one day I pulled up outside a large grocer's shop in Torquay and ordered an egg. 'Just one egg sir?' the pretty young assistant asked. 'Yes please,' I said, 'it's only to put in the radiator.' The young lady nearly burst out laughing. By the time I was outside the shop and unscrewing the large chrome top from the radiator, there were three or four assistants looking out of the window, watching me despatch this egg where no egg had ever been seen to go before! Needless to say, it didn't stop the leak and probably caused the engine to boil up even more, because it clogged up the whole radiator. On Fridays I would drive straight back from Torquay, as fast as I could. In summer, all the weekend visitors would be arriving, ready for the Friday and Saturday evening knees-up at the Hop Pole.

One of the friends I made at the Hop Pole was a gentleman called Murray Jones, sales manager of the B. French Ltd store in Kidderminster, with whom I had worked when I had been with Hoover. He was a lovely man and used to come in, dressed very smartly and usually wearing a bright yellow waistcoat, on Saturday nights. He would go round chatting to all my customers, asking if everything was satisfactory, just as though he owned the place. While this was happening I was serving pints as fast as I could, also dashing to and from the cellar carrying cases of bottled beer and lemonade. I'm sure lots of people really thought Murray was the owner and I was just the barman. My tenancy of the Hop Pole ended when, one day, Murray and I hit on the idea of opening another French's shop in Stourbridge. I had been at the Hop Pole for three years or so and recently my wife had given birth to our first daughter, Louise; consequently she was feeling ready to settle down, be a mother, and run a home instead of a pub.

11

French of Kidderminster

I looked around Stourbridge for suitable premises but could find nothing in the town itself; however, there was quite a nice shop a little way out of town in Enville Street, where the Stourbridge ring road now is. So I bought a house in Swiss Drive, Wordsley, and proceeded to open the electrical shop for B. French Ltd. From the outset, I realised that it was out of the way for the normal town shopper and therefore I would have to attract people to the shop. So I did a personal write-up of goods that we sold, which appeared in the *County Express* (the forerunner of the *Stourbridge News*) each week. Soon I was having people come into the shop to make purchases, saying how much they enjoyed my descriptive adverts. It should be remembered that this was still early days for electrical appliances. Sales took off to such an extent that, after just three months, we were starting to make the same amount of weekly turnover as the Kidderminster shop, and that had been in existence for many years.

It was while I was there that I had some major problems with my back, which had been troublesome since my spell down the mines. After various treatments at the hospital I was finally suspended and bound in a plaster cast, which had to be worn for three months. It did not stop me going to work each day, but it did produce quite horrified expressions on people's faces when they went to squeeze past me in the restricted space of the shop!

Things went quite smoothly for a couple of years, then I had the most horrific news: Murray Jones, who had effectively been my boss, had committed suicide. It was at the time when purchase tax, the forerunner to VAT, was quite drastically reduced in one of the April budgets. It appeared that Murray had been carrying quite a large amount of stock in the Kidderminster stores and, as people were being warned of a possible reduction in purchase tax, they were delaying making purchases, especially on large-ticket items like electrical products. Because the tax that was paid on purchases was non-recoverable, the firm stood to lose many thousands of pounds. Murray, a lovely man and very sensitive, took criticism from the board of B. French Ltd so personally that he decided to take his own life. Of course, this could not have been foreseen, so no one was blamed. The outcome was, however, that the board asked me to take his place and run the retail side of the business.

I managed to place an old Hoover friend of mind, Fred Moseley, in charge of the Stourbridge shop, and moved to Southampton to sort out the B. French Ltd shop there. The Southampton shop was in a good secondary position, having an upstairs and very large basement, but had not been very profitable for some time; I was hoping to find out why and get it back on track. It was only when I asked to have a look in the cellar that I found the reason for the lack of profits. It was absolutely full of part-exchange appliances! Apparently, the manager had been taking in goods, often allowing more than the profit margin on the appliance he was selling, and then depositing them with others in the cellar. Not exactly the way to run a successful business.

Having sorted Southampton out, I thought it the right time to open another shop nearer to Kidderminster, and soon found an empty one that looked ideal in a shopping arcade in Worcester. I advertised for and found a suitable manager, and a few weeks later the shop was up and running, so I had another one to keep a check on. The manager I had chosen, though not the dynamic salesman type, was a very hard working and sincere chap who was quite prepared to do the deliveries on all items sold while a young assistant looked after the shop. Once again, things started to take off after a week or two, and although never quite matching up to the Stourbridge and Kidderminster shops, it contributed to the profitability of the retail side of the B. French business.

It was a few months later, when I had been with B. French for about two and a half years, that I thought it might be time to open a shop of my own and started looking around for suitable, inexpensive premises. Bernard French, my boss, was a lovely gentleman to work for. He had always left me to do exactly what I wanted with the shops. Unfortunately, he and his wife had two handicapped children. My eldest daughter, Louise, had been brain-damaged at birth and was now becoming more troublesome. By the time I left B. French, I realised how difficult it must have been for Bernard and his wife when their children were in their formative years.

12

The Geoff Hill Electrical Store

The year was 1960. A friend of mine, John Osborne, who had been selling Flatly clothes dryers and other inexpensive electrical appliances from a shop in Brettell Lane, Amblecote, near Stourbridge, wanted to vacate the premises to go into partnership with his brother-in-law Geoff Tolly, who had an electrical shop opposite the 'Top Church', Dudley. The shop I took over was very tiny, with a frontage of about 14ft and a depth rather less than that; it had a slightly smaller room behind, complete with fireplace, also an outside toilet and wash-house across the small yard. Down the left-hand side of the shop, a passageway led to the rear. Halfway along the passageway, a steep flight of steps led to the upstairs, where

Geoff Hill's first shop in Brettall Lane was opened in 1960, and the first employee, seen here in the doorway, was Kitty Lissemore.

a small room faced the road, with a rather larger room to the rear of that. All this was on offer for the princely sum of £3 per week. I signed for a seven-year lease, little realising at the time that this was the move that would change the rest of my working life.

It was a very laid-back working environment in those early days. On cold days I would light a fire in the grate in the small rear room, and I had a dartboard there, where I could play against the Hoover representatives who regularly frequented the shop. There was also a small betting office across the road in Audnam, where I and one or two of them would sometimes indulge in the odd wager. There was certainly no indication of the potential that I would eventually be able to exploit from this tiny shop, in a nondescript shopping area like Brettell Lane.

Just before I left B. French Ltd, I traded in my super, silver 2.4 litre Jaguar car for a new Austin A55 van, much to the surprise of the car salesman. I had got to know the transport engineer at B. French Ltd quite well and he agreed to spray the van, giving it about seven coats of paint in the red and grey colours that I had chosen. He said it would last, and it did, because I used it for eight years for business, as well as for family use with temporary seats in the back, before eventually exchanging it.

Incidentally, I have fairly recently unearthed the original cash book from the time when I first opened this shop, Monday 31 October 1960. It made very interesting reading:

	Receipts				**Payments**		
	£	s	d		£	s	d
Mon	7	15	5	Postage		2	6
Tues	1	5	7	Cleaning Wages		9	4
Wed			7	J.A. Hill	3	10	0
Thurs	3	7	6	Drawings for self	12	0	0
Fri	84	0	5				
Sat	23	1	2				
Total	119	10	8	Total	16	1	10

These were the takings and expenditure from Geoff's first week of trading.

The takings didn't exactly set the world alight, with Wednesday being particularly dismal, but it was half-day closing in those days – if that's an excuse. 'J.A. Hill' was my father, who had been made redundant shortly before retirement age and was very excited to be part of his son's venture in the world of the self-employed.

I soon needed extra help in the shop, and was very lucky to find an attractive young lady named Kitty Lissemore, who would stay with me, doing a fantastic job, for most of the twenty years I was operating in Brettell Lane. On the sales side I started the

An evening view of Geoff Hill's first shop in Brettall Lane after it had been expanded by incorporating a vacant shop next door, 1964.

same 'personalised' adverts in the *County Express*, that I had used before at French's and was soon getting sales, most of which I would deliver at night after having been home for tea. I would often return to the shop to make a second or third delivery, sometimes as late as 9 p.m. Even at that hour, if I saw someone looking through the window, I would invite them in and would sometimes make a sale.

For hire-purchase facilities I used a small firm called Gaylord & Ferguson, based at Willenhall but, unfortunately, after some eighteen months they were taken over by a large company. This new firm tried to force me into paying all its hire-purchase charges for three years on two agreements, in cases where there had been a problem with a customer's payments after only a few months. It made me take what was the challenging step, at that time, of financing my own hire-purchase agreements. It was a move that I never looked back from. Although in the early days I had not sufficient cash to cover many long-term hire-purchase deals, most people only wanted a few months' credit and some could pay quite a large deposit. Quite soon there was enough money coming in from weekly payments to finance all the hire-purchase agreements. This I managed, as with all my business deals, by not borrowing even a penny from any bank.

I very soon realised that selling an item on hire-purchase would ultimately bring in twice the profit as selling the same for cash. I was very relaxed and trusting to customers when completing a sale, and for a long time did not bother to fill in hire-purchase agreements. I simply asked the amount they wanted to put down and what period they required the payments over, saying that I would put it all on a payment card and pop it in the post. Customers were amazed to find that they could take the goods away with them if they wished, even though they had only told me their name and address, without giving any further proof. Forty years ago you could trust people.

One Saturday a man came in to buy a television, having just moved from Liverpool. It was nearly closing time and as his wife was busy at home, unpacking, he wasn't too sure what sort of television she wanted. I immediately said, 'Take one you fancy and try it for the weekend, then pop in on Monday and let me know if your wife likes it or not.' He returned about 5 p.m. on the Monday and said, 'You're a trusting blighter aren't you, Geoff?' 'Well you've got an honest face and it was only for the weekend,' I replied. 'I don't know about the weekend,' he said, 'you never took my name and address!'

This incident started a long friendship with Ron Lowles and his family; although they moved to Exmouth many years ago, we are still friends to this day. I mention this little story to show how times have changed: today, unfortunately, everyone has to be checked out in detail by computer.

Geoff Hill's first Austin van is parked outside his now extended showroom, 1968.

It was about this time that my trusting nature let me down. I was called for jury service at Stafford Crown Court. The case in question was a quite serious one of drunken driving, in the days before the introduction of breathalyser tests. The jury discussed the case and, after an hour or so, the foreman called for a show of hands: ten guilty and two not guilty. After a further hour or so of intensive debate, a second show of hands: eleven guilty, with only me still arguing for the accused to be found innocent. Eventually, I had to capitulate and we returned to the court to deliver our verdict to the judge. It was only after this had been done that we were to learn of the prisoner's string of previous drink-driving convictions! I couldn't get out of the courtroom fast enough. Will I never learn?

Not long into my tenure of the Brettell Lane premises, I heard that a firm called the Provident Clothing Company were looking for office premises in the area, so I arranged that they could have the front room upstairs for the remarkably reasonable price of £3 per week. This meant that I now had rent-free premises for the remainder of my seven-year lease and I thought that I should be able to make a profit on that basis.

I had been there about two years when the next big break came. George Mason, the family grocery chain, decided to close the shop next door, from where they had operated for many years. It had a wider frontage than mine and was one big room instead of my two smaller ones, ideal for refrigerators and washing machines. I was able to take over the lease and knock part of the central wall down to make one big showroom, while retaining the original shop solely for televisions and 'wirelesses' as they were then called. I also acquired more upstairs storage space, enabling me to start buying cleaners, spin-dryers and lots of smaller appliances in much greater quantities, taking advantage of the special offers which most firms had from time to time.

I remember when Hotpoint had a competition to celebrate forty years of trading. If you won, you could buy forty washing machines with a 40 per cent discount instead of the usual 25 per cent. I managed to win this, but a few days later, when the forty twin-tubs and power-wringer washers arrived, they all had to be carried along the passage, up a steep flight of stairs, and into the back room. Fortunately, by then I was employing an electrician, Rick Wilson, who also did service work, appliance repairs and deliveries. You certainly needed two people to lift some of the machines; they were much more substantially built in those days than they are today.

I had only been in my enlarged showroom for about twelve months when Hotpoint staged a nationwide sales contest. The top twelve dealers and their wives or partners would be flown to Bermuda for a week! Forty years ago this was really something; so I pulled out all the stops to win, which I eventually did, although it did mean that practically every fridge or washing machine sold in the previous eight weeks had to be a Hotpoint! It really was a fantastic holiday, and my wife Lorraine was expecting our son at the time, after already having two girls. Out of the twelve winners, six took their wives and the other six took male friends or business partners. Before the week was through it became obvious to us married ones that we would never be allowed abroad on a trip again without our wives, after seeing the whale of a time the other six winners were having without their wives!

This holiday was the first of dozens that I would have over the next thirty years, with many different manufacturers, to exotic destinations. It wasn't too long afterwards that we won a Caribbean cruise with a large Birmingham electrical wholesaler, which included one of the first jumbo jet flights to America. We also had trips to Barbados, Los Angeles, Las Vegas and San Francisco; Hong Kong and China; Japan for two weeks with Sony; and also to various European countries, especially Spain and Majorca. They really were lovely holidays, because it was a chance to spend time with many other dealers from all parts of the UK, exchanging stories and experiences concerning our particular business.

On some of these overseas trips I occasionally rubbed shoulders with people from an electrical appliance buying group called Birmingham Combined Independents, or BCI, covering the Midlands area and based in Blackheath. It was only one of the twenty or more groups across the country that made up a nationwide organisation known as CIH, totalling some 850 dealers and based in large premises and stores at Salisbury. I had known of this buying group for some years, but as I didn't deal with many suppliers and was doing considerable turnover with the few I had, I was already able to get good quantity discounts on all my purchases. It was really just Sony and Philips on the brown goods (TVs, etc.), and Hoover and Hotpoint on the white goods (the washers and fridges). Initially, I did not think that I would be any better off being in the buying group; because, although they could buy in vast quantities and get larger discounts, there were substantial costs involved in running this mammoth organisation, paid for by putting a levy on all purchases made via CIH.

However, it was not always easy operating as a small sole trader. I went through a period where certain washing machine manufacturers tried selling direct to the public. This only lasted for a couple of years or so before the much more serious competition from the large, multiple electrical stores came onto the scene.

One of the first was Broadmeads, who actually had a showroom and regional offices only half a mile away in High Street, Wollaston, just up from the 'Fish' traffic lights. With their hundreds of stores, the multiples bought in such vast quantities that they would be selling to the public at prices that I was buying in at on single purchases. Therefore, in order to compete, I had to make my profit through the extra discounts given by manufacturers for quantity purchases, which was usually only a few extra per cent. There was a period when I was selling as many reconditioned washers as new ones. These were mainly Hoover, which I knew inside out and could recondition quite easily. I found a man at Halesowen who would do a good spray job for a few pounds and I could sell a reconditioned Hoovermatic twin-tub for 39 guineas (£40 19s), instead of the £103 19s that a brand new one cost.

Eventually, I decided that I might be better off joining this buying group after all, as it would give me access to a much broader range of merchandise. I also had an increasing feeling that we individual private dealers ought to be sticking together. Funnily enough, I did get on quite well with all the Broadmeads staff; often Rick Wilson and I would pop in to their small canteen to have a chat and bite to eat with them.

The day dawned when I joined the other fifty-five to sixty dealers who made up BCI and started attending the monthly meetings run by their chairman, Bert Pickford, a lovely man with a fairly small shop in the suburbs of Birmingham. I found it very beneficial because they had a very large warehouse, and if there were any particularly attractive offers from manufacturers I could purchase a large quantity of goods and store them there. They had a weekly delivery to all members and it was not too far to go to collect goods myself if I needed one or two items urgently.

After a few months I learned that CIH had a large trade show in London each year. We all had to go to see the manufacturers with whom the group dealt, hopefully to arrange some especially good buys. It was also going to be interesting for me to meet some of the people who ran this large group of which I was a part. I believe the show was held at Earls Court in those days, some twenty-five years or more ago. I met Bert Pickford almost as soon as I arrived. 'I'll introduce you to the chief buyer for CIH, Mr Roger Scott,' he said, 'and also to the chairman.' Bert introduced me to the two executives, saying, 'I'd like you to meet Mr Geoff Hill, a fairly new member of ours from Stourbridge.' Before I could say how pleased I was to be a member of CIH, Roger Scott said, 'So, you're Geoff Hill, are you – you're the one who keeps sending in these big orders for washing machines.' I couldn't believe it, I just thought I had a fairly small shop in a nondescript area called Brettell Lane, doing a slightly better job than average of selling washers, fridges and televisions.

It wasn't until I had been in the group for twelve months or so that I found I was actually doing the largest turnover of any shop in BCI in an area that covered the whole of Birmingham and Wolverhampton, Shrewsbury, Kidderminster, Dudley, Worcester, Leominster and some in mid-Wales. It was a sign of the changing times; lots of larger dealers had been taken over by one or other of the electrical chain stores and other smaller ones had been put out of business through not being able to compete. The electrical buying group was their only salvation.

There had been many changes in my home life since moving to live in Wordsley. When my eldest daughter Louise was about 2 years old, we had a second daughter, Teresa. Not long after she was born we moved from Wordsley into a larger house situated in a lovely country area between Kinver and Enville. The house was called 'West Lodge' and had lots of character and I remember paying £4,000 for it.

It was while I was living at Kinver that our son, Nigel, was born. We were made to realise by our local doctor that Louise, who was about 5 years old at the time, was suffering from brain damage sufficient for her to require care in residential accommodation for the foreseeable future, and possibly for the rest of her life. It was a terrible shock to us because, although she had been difficult to train and was often aggressive to the other two children, with her being our first child we had not quite known what to expect, hoping that she was a slow developer and would catch up as she grew older.

It was very difficult to find a suitable home for Louise, and the only option at the time was a mental institution at Great Barr, Birmingham. It really was a terrible place: I remember putting Louise into an old iron cot with bars from which all the

Geoff with daughter Louise and sister Gerry.

paint had been chewed. It was September and I vowed that we would only be leaving her there until Christmas at the latest. Fortunately, our problems were solved at the end of the year when I heard of a new school and residential facility opening at Cannock. It was obviously way outside our area, and I tried long and hard before they eventually agreed to take Louise on. We were very lucky, because it turned out to be a wonderful place and Louise is still there today, forty years later.

After about three years at Kinver, I was getting 'itchy feet' for a move again. Looking through the *Express & Star*, I spotted an advertisement for a beautiful timbered house called Tinkers Cottage in 2 acres of ground at Lawnswood, near Wordsley, only a few minutes from my shop. I went to have a look at it and discovered that the premises were not being lived in. I telephoned the estate agent, who immediately informed me that the house had been advertised inadvertently; the owner had moved to the Cotswolds and was waiting until spring before selling it because the woods were then full of daffodils. It was still only January and I was not to be put off easily. I asked if I could have the vendor's phone number and arranged with him to meet my wife and me on site. I was able to meet him at Tinkers Cottage a few days later and eventually I negotiated him down to £22,000 for a quick sale. The manager of Barclays Bank, Amblecote, a close friend of mine, thought that I was absolutely crazy to pay so much for a house. I told him that as well as being a super place to live in, I was also sure it would be a good investment over the years. I think I was probably right, because the value has increased some thirty-five times or more over the forty years that I have lived there.

Actually, there is quite a story about Tinkers Cottage, and it has been featured in one or two books. A Canadian architect, Major Kenneth Hutchinson Smith, who originally came to England with the army during the First World War, built the house in 1934. He also re-created some fifty or so other individual houses in Tudor style across the West Midlands during the 1920s and '30s. To do this, he bought materials and artefacts from old Tudor manor houses that were being demolished. With great skill and using specialist craftsmen, he utilised the original beams, old oak doors and flooring, leaded windows and all manner of original features to create his 'Tudor' masterpieces. Tinkers Cottage had originally been thatched, but the thatch caught fire in 1951 and it was reroofed with old tiles. It was described in one book as being, 'An exceptional Mock Tudor property of some great and unusual character'. I have always loved the place.

I was going to sell my house at Kinver for £6,000, but a friend suggested I try for £7,000. So I changed my advert in the local weekend newspaper and had a couple of decorators give it a fresh coat of Snowcem white masonry paint. I also bought a few pounds worth of daffodils in flower to fill the pots by the front door. It all looked a picture. I was working in the shop when the adverts came out. On the first day we had three different people all wanting to buy it! It became the fourth property that I had sold without using the services of an estate agent; not one had posed a problem for me.

I had also never been very keen on paying insurance premiums, unless they were obligatory by law. That probably started when I opened my initial shop in Brettell Lane. The insurance agent called and started to tell me about all the bars, grilles and other security measures that I would be obliged to install; in addition, I would have

Tinkers Cottage, Lawnswood, Wordsley, 2005. Geoff's much-loved house for forty years.

to pay a sizeable premium which would be adjusted upwards on a regular basis. I was not impressed; I had not got room to have vast amounts of stock and had about two weeks' turnover value in store at that time. I thought that if I were going to spend all the money he had suggested on security it would be like Fort Knox, so I was quite prepared to take the risk. For added measure, I also put a large sign on the back door saying, 'These Premises are Secured with High Voltage Security Equipment – You have been Warned!' It worked like a charm, and in twenty years no one ever tried to break in via the back door, although I did have a couple of burglaries at the front during the early hours. Not much stock was taken and each robbery only represented a loss equivalent to one year's insurance premium.

The next few years were reasonably uneventful on the business front, but on the home side my marriage to Lorraine was beginning to have problems. After twenty-six years she left with Nigel, Teresa and our Dalmatian dog, to set up home in a house that I had bought for her at Kinver. This was a very unhappy time of my life. Coming home to an empty, silent house at 6.30 in the evening, then having to start to cook a meal was not my scene at all. I have never considered myself to be much of a loner, and would read the newspaper for a few minutes, play the organ for a while, look at television till I was bored, then look at my watch to find it was only 8.30 p.m. or so. Occasionally, I would visit a friend to break the monotony and, of course, I played golf Wednesday afternoons and Sunday mornings, but I had never had the spare time to have other outside interests and I now realised that I would have to do something about it.

One day it suddenly occurred to me that as I was advertising to get customers each week, why couldn't I do the same thing to find someone to spend time with socially. I placed a small advertisement in the *Express & Star*, something that was not done thirty years ago. I was astounded and, in a way, quite saddened to receive some fifty replies. Saddened because it made me realise how many people there were out there who were so desperate that they would meet up with a complete stranger. With some difficulty I narrowed the choice down to half a dozen or so, and when I met Sue Billingham, from Bobbington, we got on like a house on fire from the very beginning. Crazy as it seems, she moved in to live with me not much more than two weeks later. Sue had been married before and had a 10-year-old son, Richard, but she had been divorced for many years and was as shocked as I was to find such a perfect relationship. She had been self-employed as a mobile hairdresser for years, but I found that she had trained as a beauty therapist and electrolysist. I persuaded Sue that it would better for her to pursue a career in beauty work. After a spell in Kidderminster, opening a beauty salon for a man there, we made arrangements for Sue to work from home and for her clients to come to her at Tinkers Cottage. Some two years later we had the most wonderful wedding and honeymoon.

We were brought down to earth only three months later, when a lump that I had in one of my testicles suddenly became very painful. I went straight to my doctor on the Friday morning. The doctor said it required urgent attention, and managed to arrange an appointment for me to see a consultant the very next morning at his clinic in Dudley. The consultant immediately sent me to the Guest Hospital for

Sue and Geoff outside the Methodist Church, Kingswinford, on their wedding day, 4 September 1978.

X-rays, telling me to bring them straight back to him, which I did. He said that I needed an operation, arranging for it to take place the following Monday. The most worrying factor was that I had been examined by the same consultant some months previously and had pointed out the lump; it was very small at the time and he had dismissed it as being nothing to worry about.

The operation duly took place and the testicle was removed; I was discharged from hospital next day, albeit a bit groggy. On Friday morning the phone rang to convey the news that we had both been dreading – it was a malignant cancer. I would have to go to the Royal Hospital, Wolverhampton daily for six weeks to have sessions of cobalt radiation treatment. Twenty-eight years ago to be told you had cancer was more of a death sentence than it would be today, particularly when you knew you had been walking around with it for several months. Fortunately, I am a fairly logical person and it didn't take me long to realise that nothing was to be gained by worrying or feeling sorry for myself. If it was going to be a short life, let's make it a good one and make every day count; that was my motto.

Each day I would get up and go to the shop at the usual time, then, at lunchtime Sue would run me over to the Royal Hospital for my treatment. The first day my body reacted violently and I kept trying to be sick for hour after hour. A friend of ours who was a plastic surgeon at Wordsley Hospital came and gave me special medication, but unfortunately that didn't work; in the early hours Sue had to get an emergency doctor to come out to settle my body down. The next day I went over to the hospital early to see the cancer specialist. He immediately halved the dose of cobalt treatment for the first week so that my body could gradually become used to it; thereafter it was fine. I used to go to the shop in the morning, Sue would take me over to Wolverhampton for treatment at about 2.30 p.m., then we just had time to play about six holes of golf on the way home at Enville, before I went off into my sick mode at about 7 p.m.

Throughout all these traumatic weeks Sue was brilliant and very positive; it must have seemed strange for all the other quiet, pale-faced patients waiting for treatment to see us two recent-weds laughing and joking each day as though we hadn't a care in the world! Whatever it was, it worked for me, for, although after eighteen months, sadly, I lost one of my old school friends whom I had met on my three-monthly check-ups, I survived the five years of monitoring without any further problems – I was one of the lucky ones.

Notable happenings in the next few years were my appointing Rex Hough, previously a television engineer and salesman for Regis Electric of Wordsley, to look after the brown goods side of the business, and a bright young lady, Linda Cartwright, to help with hire-purchase monitoring and sales when the showroom was busy. Everything seemed to have settled down into a fairly regular routine. I had tentatively considered on many occasions to whether I should be thinking of opening other shops in surrounding areas, but I could see myself dashing round from one shop to another. The old adage of 'if you want a job done right, do it yourself' prevailed, so I plodded on in Brettell Lane.

All this was suddenly blown out of the window when the gentleman who owned and ran Dennis Garage, a car showroom in High Street, Amblecote, 100yd away on the main road towards Stourbridge, came into my shop one day to say that he was closing down his showroom. Would I be interested in taking over the premises? Wow! This was seriously interesting because, although I had often thought I should be looking for larger premises, I had built up quite a reputation in the Amblecote area over twenty years. I had not wanted to move from this spot to start all over again in a showroom in another area. Furthermore, premises there cost only a fraction of the price that they would in a town, or even in an out-of-town shopping centre, which in those days were just starting to appear.

I immediately went to look at what seemed at the time to be vastly spacious premises. However, it took no time at all to come to a deal and arrange a moving-in date. The showroom was about 4,000sq ft and there was also a sizeable garage at the back. I decided to partition the showroom off, keeping the rear half and the garage for stores and the large frontage for the showroom. There was a nice, large window on the left-hand side in King William Street, but although windows make the shop look good they are a waste of space when it comes to racking a shop to display the largest possible amount of merchandise. So it had to be bricked up.

Once we had made the move, over a long weekend, it was so lovely to have all the stock in one big area, instead of in the rabbit warren of small rooms spread over the two shops that I had previously occupied, plus all the odd buildings that I had squeezed into behind the premises, including one over a neighbouring shop's backyard that I had covered and made into a store.

About this time both Nigel and Teresa had come back to live with us at Tinkers Cottage. Nigel worked well in the showroom, until disappearing on a world trip for two years, returning overland from Australia on a motor bike that I had to ship out to him. Since then he has only lived at home sporadically, and for the last seven years has lived in California. His world travels eventually changed his character by taking him away from the materialistic things of life such as electrical appliances, and more into carpentry work in a country setting. I think he thought I was crazy, working as hard as I did when I obviously had enough to live on comfortably. I must admit there have been odd times when I have thought that he could be right. Around 1985 Teresa fell in love with an American who was visiting this country, finally married him and went to live in Utah. She had five lovely children, but unfortunately the marriage broke up some years ago and these days she shares the custody of them. We now have plenty of excuses to visit the United States and to enjoy some of the beautiful scenery there.

Sue's son, Richard, used to like to come and help us on Saturdays when he was still at school. One day when we were particularly busy he offered to make tea for us all. He had never made tea at home, but had seen me make cups of a very weak tea that we enjoy, by holding the tea bag in the cup and pouring hot water through it. I

Geoff with son Nigel on a Californian beach.

Geoff's daughter Teresa (centre) with her family. Left to right: Mitchell, Brittanie, Brooke and Elliot, with Brieya in front.

would make a second and sometimes even a third cup with the same tea bag in this way. You can imagine what happened when he tried to make fourteen cups of tea with one tea bag, proudly bringing them through to us in the showroom! He was only about 12 at the time but, like Nigel, he started to work in the showroom after he had left school. He was a very pleasant and kind sort of lad – too kind in some ways, because we would discover strangers standing about in our stores, only to find that they had delivered something and Richard had asked them in there while he made them a cup of coffee. Not exactly the high security level that we liked our hundreds of thousands of pounds worth of stock to be kept in! On another occasion we were short of one of the delivery vans, only to find that Richard had lent it to a friend who was moving house. Sue and I talked things over and decided it might be good for Richard to go out and get a job for himself, so that he would be working somewhere where he had to toe the line more. Hoping that the experience would do him good, we thought that we could then have him back again later. Imagine our surprise when, a day or two later, he landed a job at the Mothers Pride bakery adjacent to our showroom, working four nights per week and being paid about twice as much as we had paid him!

When I had my cancer scare, Sue finished with her beauty work and came to help at the showroom, ostensibly to help me with the bookkeeping work. As she often related afterwards, she transferred from one lot of figures to another! Unfortunately, the second lot she didn't enjoy at all; in fact, she was a brilliant sales lady and was out of the office and onto the showroom floor, talking to customers, at every opportunity.

When I moved premises, the new showroom had a large triple-window frontage, and often people stood outside in the rain, getting soaked. I thought a long canopy would solve the problem, but the estimate I received for one this big and of a good quality was enormous; however, I thought there would be good advertising capacity in such a thing because we were on a busy main road. I worked out the appropriate costs and approached half a dozen of my main suppliers, all of whom accepted the idea. A week or two later I not only had a beautiful canopy for free, but had also made an extra £500 into the bargain! As the old saying goes, 'there's more than one way to skin a cat'.

During 1984 my accountants advised me that it would be more beneficial for me to become a limited company, so from 1 June of that year 'Geoff Hill' was no more; I was now trading as 'Geoff Hill Limited'. It was about the same time that I wondered if there would be a chance of acquiring an in-store demonstrator, such as Beatties and Rackhams had at the time. Hotpoint seemed the most likely company

The Geoff Hill Electrical Store staff outside the showroom after the new brown advertising canopy had been fitted, 1988.

to try, as I did a considerable turnover with them. I discovered that my turnover was as much, if not more than, Beatties' store at Wolverhampton. When I first proposed the idea to my Hotpoint representative, he said quite emphatically, 'Sorry, Geoff, we never put demonstrators in private shops, only in large stores.' I wasn't prepared to accept this, especially as I was doing enough turnover to warrant one, so I insisted on taking it up with senior management. The final outcome was that I was allocated a very nice lady from Kidderminster, three days a week, free of charge. Yippee!

A month or two later I thought what I had done with Hotpoint I could try with Zanussi. After stressing to their representative how sales would drop unless we could have a Zanussi demonstrator for three days per week, I managed to get them to supply one as well; not long after that, by the same method, I obtained a Hoover demonstrator too! I insisted they all wear Geoff Hill uniforms, also asking them not to push their own product if the customer quite definitely preferred their own choice of appliance. It worked very well and the girls got on famously together, often selling a washer or fridge for each other while on lunch breaks.

Microwaves were becoming popular at the time, costing a few hundred pounds apiece in the early days. People simply didn't know how they worked, so they had to be demonstrated too. I soon managed to get a Panasonic demonstrator to alternate with a Sharp lady at weekends. I also started having microwave demonstration evenings in the Methodist Church Hall just across the road from the showroom. We would serve coffee and biscuits and have a hundred or more people in there; the demonstrator would cook a whole table full of food in an hour or so and we would then go round, sampling the food, and hopefully taking orders. We also did some demonstrations at the Pedmore House Hotel, and I remember that one night so many people turned up we couldn't get them all into the room, so we hurriedly arranged a second demonstration for the same time the following week. I also had a Vax cleaner demonstrator for a limited time; in fact, half the people selling on the shop floor were unpaid staff. They were great times, but unfortunately, as the years went by, trading became more difficult for manufacturers, especially with cheaper models coming in from the Far East, and eventually all the demonstrators were withdrawn.

Early in 1991 I was offered the opportunity to purchase the premises. This I did, and on the advice of my accountant I rented it out to the Geoff Hill Limited company. For some years we had been desperately short of storage space, especially over the Christmas period, which is the busiest time of the year, and every one of the suppliers, including CIH, our own buying group, shut down for two to three weeks. It was later in 1991 that I was able to purchase a small piece of land across the road in King William Street, just large enough to build a store capable of holding all the Hotpoint items, sometimes a little more.

On the staff side, once it became obvious that my son Nigel would not take any part in the business, Robert, my half-brother, was promoted to work alongside me, learning just how hard it is to run a large, successful operation such as this. It needs a great deal of dedication and application, qualities that fortunately, like me, he seems to have inherited from our father. Robert became a director, as did Rex Hough, who had run the television side of the business. An old school friend of Nigel's, Bob Billingham, who, although still reasonably young, showed considerable

The Geoff Hill Gas and Electrical Superstore in High Street, Amblecote, as it is today.

potential, was also made a director. A little later Linda Cartwright, who had been monitoring the ever-increasing accounts side of the business, was made our financial director. They were all appointments that worked exceedingly well for the company, and although I only had quarterly board meetings, they became progressively longer and can now last up to four hours!

I had always employed wonderful staff and I thought it would be nice for them to have a share in the business, so shares were issued to all staff, with allocations based on their salary, new employees also qualifying after three years' service. Dividends are paid before Christmas, along with a sizeable Christmas bonus. When members of the staff leave, their shares are bought back by the company. It has been said that this is one reason that I have such good staff, but I disagree: we go to endless trouble at interviews to try to get people with pleasant personalities as well as the needed capabilities to sell a vast range of merchandise. A considerable amount of product training is carried out, and I receive countless comments praising the staff for their expert knowledge of so many different appliances.

By the late 1980s I was beginning to have enough time on my hands to become a director of our local buying group BCI, which was becoming increasingly important to our competitive purchasing and the storage of our extra stock. Instead of doing all the buying and seeing representatives at the Geoff Hill store, as I had done over the years, my brother Robert was now buying in all the major white goods, Bob looking after the small appliances, and Rex in charge of the brown goods, TVs etc. By 1990 I had decided to ease myself out of the day-to-day running of the business for pastures new, and just remain as chairman.

In 1997 we managed to squeeze quite a few more feet of showroom space out of our land-locked site by building an extension across the whole front of the showroom, moving the entrance from the High Street into King William Street. It was carried out over the Christmas period and was at times a bit traumatic, but it did transform the front of the showroom, both internally with the extra space and externally by bringing the showroom and illuminated fascia much closer to the main road. The protrusion of the new building also gave us a useful wall, on the side approached from Stourbridge, to use for display purposes. This is very much the Geoff Hill store as it is today, staffed by some twenty-five super people (I have been told that so many times since coming out of the business), always dressed in smart uniforms. I introduced one or two different business slogans over the years; the one which seemed to stand the test of time was, 'Best prices. Best service. Best deliveries.'

Deliveries were always carried out within 24 hours, unless the customer required the goods on a specific day. We have often arrived at the customer's house with their purchases before they themselves had returned from the shop! Years ago, when people came some distance by bus, we sometimes took them home along with the goods they had just purchased. Nowadays, people who have dealt with us for years sometimes just phone to tell us their washer or fridge has broken down, leaving it to us to send the most appropriate replacement appliance and paying on delivery. I think it says a lot when people have that much trust and respect for our judgement and reputation. I have always been a bit of a perfectionist in business matters – that, coupled with accountancy and statistical interests have, I feel, proven invaluable assets throughout my business life.

During the last few years, we have entered competitions to find the dealer with the best customer service. In 2003 we entered one, promoted by the *Express & Star* and Black Country Chamber of Commerce, to find the best dealer in any category in the whole of the Black Country area, and eventually ended as runners-up to a large Wolverhampton wholesaler. In 2004 we entered a national competition to find the best electrical retailer, in a competition open to all types, including branches of Comet, Currys, etc. We were surprised to find that we again won the runners-up spot. I think it's something the store staff can all be proud of!

Talking of staff, I have had several super staff who have now been with me for over twenty years. Sadly, early in 2006 one of them, a very popular lad called Shaun Cox, decided to leave because he could get a better job with one of our suppliers, where he would not have to work at weekends. When I presented an appropriately engraved wristwatch to him on his departure, he made a short but very moving speech. He said that every day he came to the showroom since he first joined us on a government Youth Training Scheme all those years ago, he never felt that he was coming to work, he enjoyed the staff and the customers so much.

'To me', he said, 'I start my working life next Monday!'

Not many employers hear those kinds of words from their staff I'm sure.

These days I just drop into the showroom once or twice a week to collect mail and have a quick chat. I remain chairman of Geoff Hill Limited and the Geoff Hill Charitable Trust, more of which I will tell you about later. Keith Hough (televisions, hi-fi, etc.) is managing director of Geoff Hill Limited, with my wife Sue, Linda Cartwright (accounts) and Lee Smart (washers, refrigerators, etc.) making up the remainder of the board.

13

The Mary Stevens Hospice Fundraising

It wasn't until late in 1989, and approaching the 30th anniversary of the opening of my shop in Brettell Lane, that I thought about celebrating it in some way. I had been invited to another business's 'Champagne Breakfast' in Stourbridge, a few months earlier, but that didn't seem the way to go for me. Over the years I had been involved in donating prizes to lots of local charities for raffles and tombolas, and I thought it would be more appropriate to do something along those lines. Eventually, I decided to give away thirty colour televisions to local charities and needy causes, which they could then use as prizes in their raffles during the run-up to Christmas. I knew there would be a lot of applicants, so I hired the Methodist church hall across the road and announced the event in the local free newspapers, adding that they would have to attend the actual draw to stand a chance of winning a free television set.

To make it more of a fun night, I thought it might be nice to have Tommy Munden, the Black Country comedian, come along; so I gave him a ring to see if he was free that evening. I said, 'Oh, hello, Tommy, this is Geoff Hill here.' It seemed to go quiet, so I added, 'I've got an electrical store in Amblecote.' 'Yer silly sod!' he retorted. 'Every bugger knows yoe,' he said in a typical Tommy fashion, also adding that he would be delighted to help on the night. We were off to a great start.

The big night soon came around. By then some seventy-five charities and needy causes had written to be present on the night. To save too many being disappointed, I spoke to some of my major television suppliers and managed to have five extra sets donated, in addition to the thirty portables that we had mounted in a large pyramid on the stage. My staff served tea, coffee and biscuits to the 130 or so people who were seated in the hall, waiting for the proceedings to begin. I introduced Tommy Munden, who really needed no introduction, to get everyone in a laughing mood before I began the serious stuff.

I noticed an old school friend of mine from King Edward's sitting in the front row, who had come along to represent the Mary Stevens Hospice, which, at the time, was still only an aspiration and had not yet been built. Before starting the big draw I welcomed everybody and, quite impromptu, said, 'I hope none of you will mind, but I have a very old friend of mine here from our school days representing Mary Stevens Hospice, and as I feel we desperately need the services of one in the

Stourbridge area, I would like to donate this large Sony television set to him.' Everyone applauded as Jim Higgs stepped forward to receive the wonderful 27in stereo, teletext model that Sony had kindly donated for the evening. The rest of the night went very well. I invited people to say a few words about their particular charity if they wished, and as we were all charity-minded it was interesting to hear what they had to say. I tended to be the 'straight man' for Tommy's humorous comments, and about two hours later the last television was drawn.

Only Jim, his wife Pat, Sue, Tommy and I, were left in front of the stage. 'What's the best thing to do with this television, Geoff?' said Jim, who was a lovely person – not your 'hands on' fundraiser, but a perfect chairman for the Hospice fundraising groups. Before I could reply, Tommy said, 'Book the Civic Hall at Brierley Hill and I'll bring the Black Country Entertainers along free of charge and we can raffle Geoff's TV off on the night!' That's just what we did, and I think we raised some £2,000 during the evening to add to the Hospice fund coffers.

Not long afterwards I started approaching my many suppliers to donate items for prizes in order that a large raffle could be staged in aid of the Hospice. I had always had a very good relationship with all the firms and their representatives, so prizes soon started rolling in and eventually I had seventeen electrical appliances: televisions, videos, washers, fridges, dishwashers, hi-fis – you name it, we had it. The total retail value was over £2,500, so I realised that we had to sell a great many raffle tickets just to cover those wonderful gifts. I had to have quite large tickets printed so that the details of the goods and their donors could appear, and decided to price them at only 25p each so that everyone could afford to have a go.

My initial order was for 10,000 so that if all tickets were sold it would produce £2,500. We needed something special to give a kick-start to the ticket sales, so I decided to donate a television for the person selling the most, with two runner-up prizes of stereo radio cassettes. It worked like a dream, and people were coming in to collect raffle tickets, selling them, and then coming back for more. In no time the tickets were flying out so, optimistically, I ordered another 10,000.

My wife, Sue, also rose to the challenge. In the evenings she went around houses, pubs, clubs – you name it, she went there, selling her tickets. Sometimes she would enrol a friend to go with her, but more often than not she went on her own. I was left at home filling in the hundreds of counterfoils, because she would often sell £5, £10, or even £20 worth on some occasions at the larger houses. To save time, she would only complete the first counterfoil with the name and phone number if she sold £20 worth to one person – I had the other seventy-nine to fill in when she got home! I was soon wishing that I had charged more for the tickets. The second 10,000 sold out, then a third 10,000 came and went. Finally, 32,000 tickets were sold, making it what was billed in the local newspaper as, 'The biggest raffle ever held in Stourbridge!' As I had both supplied the prizes and footed the bill for the printing, I had a tidy sum of £8,000 ready to hand over to the Hospice.

To swell the funds even more, Sue and I arranged a Grand Draw Night, to be held in our garden. We invited lots of friends round and laid on a tombola and other fundraising ideas. Brian Marshall, chairman of the Hospice, and Jim Higgs helped me to draw the prize-winners out of a giant television box full of counterfoils. We also presented prizes to the ticket sellers. The father of two of my staff sold the most tickets, £510 worth, closely followed by the runners-up who sold £450 and £440 each. Sue, incidentally, sold over £700 worth and thoroughly enjoyed herself in doing so, far more than I, who night after night had been filling in her blessed counterfoils. We made a considerable amount of money on the night and I rounded it up to £1,000, so that a few days later £9,000 was winging its way to the Hospice.

It was not long after this that Sue and I formed the Wordsley Fundraising Group. We started off with half a dozen stalwarts from the church at Wordsley: Noel and Barbara Hughes (for many years promoters of Wordsley Carnival), Chris and Mike Leashorne, and Trevor and Mary Tipton, all very experienced at fundraising for the church. We added to this assemblage when Sue and I were at Dudley Town Hall one night, attending a Gentleman Songsters evening that had been held jointly in aid of the Mayor's Charity and Mary Stevens Hospice. At the end of the evening, the Mayor and I went on the stage to express our respective thanks to everyone; at the same time I said that if anyone present would like to help with Hospice fundraising they should see me afterwards. It worked well because Mike Baker, one of the organisers of the Gentleman Songsters, offered to help, along with his wife, Hazel. Our group was made up with Rob Newey, our local butcher, and later with a friend of mine from Dudley Hospital Radio, Geoff Wakeman, and also John Robinson. We not only raised a great deal of money, but in the process had a lot of fun. I was chairman and Sue was secretary and treasurer. Sometimes meetings held at our house would become so uproarious that I would be compelled to bang the table and shout 'Order, order!' Mike Leashorne would retort, 'I'll have a pint and Chris a gin and tonic.' The meeting would disintegrate into laughter and the back-chatting started again.

I thought it would be a good idea, during the run-up to Christmas, to have a dance at the Stourbridge Town Hall, so I booked the last Saturday in November, making sure the decorations were in place for that date. It was billed as the Geoff Hill Big Band Dance, and we hired Bobby Johnson and His Band, who were the star attraction at the time. The hall held 300 people seated in tables of ten, and to make the event a real money-spinner we were determined to fill every table, which we did. To raise a few extra pounds, I decided to hold a large raffle during the first interval, normally raising over £500, and then in the second, short, interval do a quick auction of some twelve or so items. We ran the dance with this format for the next eight years, a sell-out on every occasion.

The day of the dance was always manic. In the morning we were chasing around, collecting the bread, tomatoes, cheese, ham, sausage rolls and pork pies that usually constituted the food served during the interval. At lunchtime the fundraising group would meet at Wordsley church hall and in about an hour and a half we had plated and cello-wrapped some 320 meals for the dancers, band and Town Hall staff. At 6 p.m. we were at the Town Hall, decorating tables with coloured tablecloths, flowers, serviettes, bowls of crisps and Hospice notices. As soon as the doors opened we were welcoming everyone and sorting out cash, Sue noting the telephone numbers of any new dancers so that they could be contacted the following year. During the interval we would be selling raffle tickets and serving food. When the interval was over we would be folding raffle tickets and counting money, so that

Geoff receives a cheque for £2,000 for the Mary Stevens Hospice from Black Country author Stan Hill, the profit from his book on Brierley Hill, 2001.

when I did the draw I could also announce exactly how much had been made on the night.

Following the draw, I did the auction. After that it was all added together so that I could give a grand total at the end of the evening. Sue and I both love dancing, but a quick rock and roll, followed by the last waltz, was usually about all we could manage. After talking to lots of people and clearing the tables, we eventually staggered home, shattered. Oh, and by the way, I nearly forgot to mention that we usually raised somewhere in the region of £3,000 on the night, so I guess it was all worthwhile.

We instigated another major fundraising event that was to run for many years. Sue and I started the Hospice Fête in 1992 in a field adjacent to Hurrans Garden Centre, on the Kidderminster Road running out of Hagley. We encouraged all the Hospice fundraising groups to take a stall each. The Wordsley group had a giant tombola stall with literally hundreds of prizes which the Leashornes and Tiptons ran with their usual 'market trader' chat, and the newly opened Stourbridge Hospice shop displayed items it had been collecting specially for the occasion. To complete the scene, I had been fortunate in making contact with a David Spruce and his father, Bob, who arranged to bring a selection of vintage vehicles over from the Bridgnorth Vintage Vehicle Club. We also ran a large raffle and, although the weather was not too kind for June, we made about £2,000, at the same time giving the Hospice some much-needed publicity with posters and road signs.

In July 1993 we held a second Hospice Fête on the same site. This time we had, in addition, some trade stalls on which we negotiated a percentage of takings for the Hospice. There was also a separate Dog Show, organised by a friend of ours, Ann Preston, a breeder of Great Danes, one of which was our pride and joy. We added a bouncy castle for the children and, blessed with better weather, we raised rather more than the £2,000 of the previous year.

We had started to run out of room on the fête ground and my eyes turned to a much larger field of about 11 acres right opposite Hurrans, owned by Lord Cobham. After one or two phone calls it was arranged that we could have the use of this field free of charge, and we managed also to have it mown a few days in advance of the fête. The day before the fête was usually pretty hectic, obtaining stakes and ropes to create a performing area, with tables and chairs for people to sit at for their lunchtime snacks. This year one of the committee members, butcher Rob Newey, had offered to do a 'pig roast'. In addition, there was also a large brass band, and miniature train rides for the children. The larger field provided much more room for the vintage vehicles and engines, so a vast array of interesting items had been assembled, helping to fill the extra space.

The Stourbridge Lions also began to do food for us at lunchtime, we had the Cider House vehicle and an ice cream van that all helped to swell the takings. By then, the Hospital Radio crew had joined in with their roadshow and loudspeaker equipment, to help in general with announcements and music. I managed to find a printer who produced programmes for us free of charge, funding them by obtaining advertisements from a list of businesses that supported the Hospice. We were able to sell the programmes before the event for £1 each, qualifying one person for free entry on the day. All went well for us on Sunday 17 July 1994, and we ended by making just under £3,000.

The following year was to be our last at organising the fête. By then I was heavily involved in opening and running the Hospice charity shops and starting the Hospice lottery. We were more determined than ever to make it a good one and, if possible, wanted to completely fill the 11-acre field. The vintage vehicle boys were prepared to turn out in force, with over 150 vehicles, motorbikes and engines, to organise the parking and also to take the money at the gate for us. Rob Newey said he would do a big barbeque and the Lions a food stall. I arranged for a fifty-piece school band, the Karen Yates Dancers and the Bedcote Morris Men, all to perform in the

Some of the veteran and vintage cars in the 11-acre field at Hagley which was used for the Hospice Fête in July 1994.

entertainment area; with a bouncy castle, slides, roundabout, trampolines and face painting for the children, not to mention Crackers the Clown! To really fill the area, we had the Dog Show ring separately, with cups and rosettes for the winners. To get people into the showground early, we had the ever-popular car boot sale.

The week before the fête we organised a day of selling programmes in Stourbridge Ryemarket, selling close on 1,000. With others sold at the Hospice and shops, we were able to start the day with well over £1,000 in takings. Blessed with lovely weather on the day, the crowds turned out in their thousands. The day finished with us making what proved to be a record amount for the fête, £6,100. It was nice to go out on a high, and the next year we were able to pass on all the details and contacts to the Hospice fundraiser to ensure its ongoing success.

As well as the Big Band Dance and the fête we also capitalised every year on the large Wordsley Carnival, which our two fundraising members, Noel and Barbara Hughes, had run for many years. It usually encompassed two days, with a fun run the first day, followed by a procession of bedecked vehicles and the fête on the second day. Sue and I usually had a go in the fun run, sometimes with our Great Dane, Caruthers. However, it was with the procession that we usually made most of the money, with every one of our friends flashing their collection tins along the route. With help from the carnival committee, the total proceeds usually varied between £1,000 and £3,000.

We held a whole succession of events over the years, featuring the Amblecote Singers, Kidderminster Male Voice Choir, the Ellenvale Singers and Gentleman Songsters, at Brierley Hill Civic Hall, Dudley and Stourbridge Town Halls, and King Edward's College at Stourbridge. With the aid of James Morgan, a Wollaston estate agent, we also had an enjoyable Peter Skellern concert that raised over £2,000, and lots of smaller jazz nights and skittle evenings. Each Christmas we had

Geoff and Sue at Wordsley carnival, 1993.

Elizabethan fun at George Wood's house-opening fundraising weekend in 1993. Left to right: Garry Moore, Sue, George Wood (jester) and Geoff.

a big collection at Merry Hill, sometimes with the Salvation Army Band, and that would raise another £1,000 or so.

There were a few slightly different fundraising events along the way. One was in 1993, when a lady who ran an Elizabethan troupe phoned. She had about twenty people in the troupe who did courtly dances of the period, all in costume and to the music of that era. That was the easy bit; what we had to do was to find an appropriate venue with seating, organise food and, last but by no means least, sell the tickets. We eventually settled on Blakelands at Bobbington, where there was a large barn that had recently been renovated. Although very different, we had an enjoyable evening that, once again, raised a few hundred pounds for the Hospice.

It was in the same year that the quite zany builder friend of mine who lives next door, George Wood, was completing a large, mock-Tudor house, which looked very imposing and was beautifully finished inside with exposed beams, large open fireplaces and a minstrel gallery. What made it a great point of interest to local people was that, in order to build it, he had demolished a lovely four-bedroomed house that he had only built some sixteen years previously! I could see that holding an 'open house' there would have serious fundraising potential, and sowed the seeds of the idea to George. I don't think he was too keen at first, but after a week or two he popped round to give us the go-ahead.

As it happened, that year the girls at my electrical store had arranged for the staff Christmas party to be in fancy dress and held in the dungeons of Warwick Castle. Sue and I had already booked our costumes as Anne Boleyn and Henry VIII, and as the party was on a Friday night we would still have them for the following Saturday and Sunday. We just had enough time to advertise it heavily, get George and his son

Geoff in cavalier fancy dress on the oak staircase at Tinkers Cottage, 1995.

Marcus fixed up with medieval outfits, help to clean the house ready for the opening, and then we were ready. I managed to borrow some large silver punchbowls, and Sue and I served mulled punch and mince pies as people entered the house. The lady who had previously staged the Elizabethan evening brought her troupe along each day to dance for us, and also played tapes of Elizabethan music to provide the appropriate atmosphere. We must have had about 1,000 people through the house over the weekend, and after paying for the mince pies and wine, we had made just over £2,000 on what I'm sure was a most unusual fundraising event.

The last fundraising event that I want to write about revolved around Enville Golf Club, where I had been a member for twenty-five years or so until I retired from the Geoff Hill business. 'Until you retired from business?' I hear you ask. 'Surely that is when you play four or five times a week instead of the occasional weekday and Sunday.' 'Not in my case,' I reply. You see, I was one of the very unusual breed that gives up golf entirely to concentrate on fundraising, which by then had become a full-time occupation.

By 1994 we had a paid fundraiser, Gerald Wood. One day he suggested it might be an idea to put on a Golf Day at Enville Golf Club to raise money for the Hospice. I said I had a better idea that I had wanted to implement for some time. The idea was to have a qualifying golf competition for both ladies and gentlemen at all the five or six clubs in the catchment area of the Hospice. The top five from each club, and their respective captains, would compete against each other in the final. The first year it was to be held at Enville Golf Club, moving the following years around the other clubs in turn. In my experience golfers were quite generous people, and as well as earning money for us on a regular yearly basis, it would also help to publicise the Hospice right across the borough. I offered to buy trophies for both the ladies' and gentlemen's winning teams, which would have the names of the clubs engraved on the base; I would also supply medals for every member of the winning teams. In October 1994 we held the first competition at Enville Golf Club, receiving a massive £6,000 from the clubs that year. Since then I have had medals engraved and we have received over £3,000 each year from the clubs. They all look forward to the competition.

By 1997 Sue and I were getting heavily involved in sourcing and selling Christmas cards, also opening and running charity shops. By then I was also

Geoff receives a cheque for £1,912 for the Mary Stevens Hospice from Val McCready, ladies' captain, Hagley Golf Club.

involved in starting the Hospice lottery. Something had to go, and it had to be the fundraising group. I think the others, too, were ready to 'move on' by then. We had worked hard for six years, in which time we had raised well over £100,000, having had a great deal of fun in the process of doing it.

We continued for a year or two with staging the Big Band Dance in the run-up to Christmas, but it was a particularly busy time for us, distributing and selling anything up to 90,000 Christmas cards, so eventually that had to be handed over to another fundraising group. The last few years we had the services of the Perfect Timing band, run by Jim and Kay Harcourt, who, coincidentally, helped Sue and me at Tinkers Cottage. We still get a Christmas card from a dear couple at Cookley, saying how much they miss our Big Band Dance. It was sad for us to read at Christmas 2002 that the Stourbridge Town Hall Dance had had to be cancelled at short notice because only fifty tickets had been sold.

Over the years we had regular meetings at the Hospice of representatives of its fundraising groups. Jim Higgs chaired these meetings in the early years and we had nine or ten groups represented from across the borough, but unfortunately never one from Dudley; for some reason we never made much headway with fundraising in this area. When Gerald Wood took over as our paid fundraising coordinator, he started to chair the meetings and I had become a Hospice board member. I had also started the trading company and lottery, and so was able to give everyone attending (invariably all ladies) an update on these three different aspects of the Hospice. It was, quite honestly, very surprising to me that over the years, as it has developed in supplying its specialised care to more and more people across the borough, the number of fundraising groups diminished and we were down to just five when I left the Hospice.

I had a letter in February 1992 from William Stewart, fundraising coordinator at St Anne's Hospice, Manchester, inviting me to attend an Inaugural National Hospice Fundraisers' Conference to be held there on 12 May. I went with Jim Higgs and was surprised to find representatives from most hospices in the United Kingdom. It was a full programme from 10 a.m. to 4 p.m., with various speakers, including Martyn Lewis of the BBC, who had always been interested in the hospice movement. It was very well received by all, and the idea of working together at national and regional levels was born.

National fundraising conferences were to follow annually, with regional ones held every few months. The regional conferences proved to be very useful in those early

Sue and Geoff with the Perfect Timing band, which they engaged for most of the eight years when they held the Geoff Hill Big Band Night at Stourbridge Town Hall, 1994.

days, when people could contribute ideas that had worked for them, for everyone else to feed off. It was also of particular interest to me, as a member of the Hospice board, to be able to have a conducted tour round so many of the other hospices in the Midlands.

I can remember visiting hospices at Birmingham, Wolverhampton, Kidderminster, Shrewsbury, Worcester, Hereford, Lichfield, Nottingham, Leicester and Milton Keynes. I went to some several times, as we later started a similar operation with hospice trading companies and, finally, lotteries. All the representatives attending these meetings were invariably paid managers for fundraising, shops or lotteries. Here was I attending all three, and not even an employee, only a volunteer. Although it was obviously hectic at times I always found it both educational and enjoyable, although some I spoke to thought I was quite mad!

We were also later to be one of a few hospices to join the National Association of Charity Shops, to which all the large chains belong. Their meetings were always held in London, but I never attended one. However, the minutes were always useful and I found it interesting, as a businessman, to see how these larger organisations performed. The feedback on health and safety issues and other legislation was also useful, because it was an ever-changing scene and this provided an up-to-date scenario of government requirements in these areas.

14

Hospice Christmas Cards

I started selling Christmas cards in a small way in 1991, purchasing the cards at a discount price from a local specialist card wholesaler that I knew. Come 1992, with the Day Hospice now up and running, I thought it time to take the sale of Christmas cards seriously. As well as providing an income for the Hospice, printed cards would bring an awareness of it that we were all desperately trying to create.

To source Christmas cards commercially you have to attend the massive Gift Fair held at the National Exhibition Centre, Birmingham, in the first week of February each year. It is the biggest exhibition held there every year; all the halls are taken, one or two of them exclusively selling cards. We soon found that only a small percentage catered for the charity trade sector by having an overprinting facility. My next task, therefore, was to find the ones on which I could maximise the profit, because although it's nice to sell vast quantities of cards – or any other goods for that matter – it is the profit margin that's important. I managed to find a firm called EMS that would do a good deal for me, although I had to buy a minimum of 5,000 of each card (10,000 with some other firms, as I was later to find out).

Suddenly, out of the blue, we had another unexpected option, when Sue's sister Ann, who dealt with artists and had produced her own range of Christmas cards for a number of years, decided to sell her entire stock of 46,000 blank cards as she was suffering from ME. She let me have them for a real bargain price, but then I had to source the cello-wrap, envelopes and backing slips, as well as having the blank cards suitably overprinted. When that was all done I had to get the cards packed into tens, which the Hospice patients and volunteers readily agreed to do. Finally, as I envisaged selling them in many different outlets, I put an extra label in the top right-hand corner: 'Mary Stevens Hospice – 10 cards – £2.95'.

They were all 8in x 6in cards, and excellent value for money. Only costing about £1 per pack, they showed the profit margin I was looking for. During the following years we usually bought from up to five different manufacturers. Therefore, each year we had to wade through hundreds of sample cards, either at the NEC, or with representatives who arranged to visit us at home. We ended up with thirty or forty samples from which we would select about fourteen for the final order.

For the first eight years I sold all the cards from my garage, stocking 50,000 after two years, then up to 75,000 in later years. It was quite a formidable task. From 1 October to the end of the year my Volvo estate car had the back seats permanently down and was filled with fifteen to twenty different types of Christmas card: children's, robins, religious, nostalgia, flowers, Santa Clauses, snow scenes, etc.

It was always important to have the correct mix of cards – and not only the ones that Sue and I would have bought! It was also important to have quite a range of differently priced cards, so I always had packs of ten cards starting from £1.75 or £1.95 for some outlets, and about four larger cards selling from £3.95 up to £4.95 per pack for businesses and the more discerning customer. I always had facilities with a local printer to get them personalised – once again, mainly for businesses, where, in one case alone, I had an order for 12,000 cards!

We spent a considerable amount of time going round different retailers and asking them to sell our Christmas cards, and eventually we built up a round of about thirty outlets, Ashwood Nurseries, Barnett Hill Nurseries and Stourbridge Library being the main ones, plus doctors' surgeries, post offices, ladies' hairdressers and lots of other places, including my own electrical store. All helped to keep them moving. It was not always as easy as you might think. I always gave a small discount to people who already sold their own range of Christmas cards, and when I encouraged Ashwood Nurseries to stock them in their gift shop, they sold so well that they were afraid of being left with many of their own unsold. Not to be put off, I suggested that they sell them near the checkout in their plant area; they kindly agreed to do this, and have sold many thousands every year since. As you can imagine, it meant calling round everyone regularly, topping up the cards and collecting the cash, but the total profit from cards was usually about £10,000.

Sue and I also put on a stall of cards, calendars, diaries and lots of other items at all Hospice fundraising events in the run-up to Christmas, as well as at the annual weekend event at the Bonded Warehouse, when we took up to £1,000. The wife of one of our trustees, Val Johnson, also opened her lovely house each year to invited friends and we would take another £1,000 there. Finally, after taking our stall around golf and ladies clubs for a year or two, we opened Tinkers Cottage, and sold about £1,500 worth of Christmas goodies each year.

After starting the Hospice Lottery in 1996, I hit on the idea of selling people a lottery ticket to enter the house, getting their coffee and biscuits free. I thought this might encourage them to become regular players of the Hospice Lottery. Incidentally, one year a ticket purchased to enter our house won the happy person the first prize of £1,000.

One of the main outlets for selling the cards was the Hospice itself, where we had two small shop areas; one in the Day Centre, the other in the Residential Unit. The other place where the cards sold well was the Stourbridge Hospice Shop, where I would top up and display the cards every Monday, Wednesday and Friday.

I remember one year, when we were still selling cards from home, I had a call from EMS saying that they had 45,000 cards to deliver the next day and were just checking this unusual address, Tinkers Cottage, and wondering if I had a fork-lift truck to handle nearly a ton of Christmas cards! I explained that the sixty or so cartons had to go into my garage and that, as the massive delivery van could not get into my drive, I would load up my Volvo estate car from the roadside eight or ten cartons at a time! It was certainly unusual, but it worked. I was probably the only charity in the country selling 75,000 cards without incurring one penny in expenditure, so that literally every last penny went to the Hospice.

15

The Mary Stevens Hospice Trading Company Ltd

It was at one of Jim Higgs's meetings of fundraising group leaders that I happened to say, 'Some of the volunteers seem to think that we should have a charity shop, Jim, don't you think it's time we did something about it?' 'Yes Geoff,' he replied, 'that's a good idea', and, quick as a flash, he added, 'Can I leave it to you to get a committee together to organise it?'

The committee turned out to be just Sue and me. We undertook visiting all the empty premises in Stourbridge, Brierley Hill, Halesowen and Dudley, assessing their potential as our Hospice shop. We eventually decided on a two-storey shop in Victoria Passage, which is situated just off the middle of Stourbridge High Street. My thinking was that it would be easy to pay for a plum position in the High Street, where one or two other charity shops were situated – but the rents were three times higher than the asking rental for this shop, which was only 10 or 15yd from the High Street.

I found out that it had been empty for a month or two, so I managed to get the asking rental down from £6,500, to only £4,000 for the first year. The upstairs had never been used at all, so I had to create a workroom and changing cubicle and areas to process clothes, and fit a sink unit, order a clothes steamer, and have it decorated and carpeted throughout. For downstairs, I found a spare counter from my own shop, and ordered the uprights and 'D' rails for the walls, as well as free-standing display stands for the clothes, plus a few extra for upstairs. I felt it needed raised window display areas, made with a storage space beneath, and two more changing cubicles. Finally, a most important piece of equipment, a till. Through the local press I requested volunteers; with my entire shop staff and fundraising group doing the same, I soon had thirty-five lovely ladies waiting and willing to give half a day or more of their time each week.

I had previously been with Sue over to Compton Hospice at Wolverhampton, to have a chat with their fundraiser as to how they operated the management of their charity shops. He told us that there were two manageresses for each shop, each doing three days per week and covering each other for sickness or holidays. This sounded a sensible arrangement, so I advertised, and found two ladies with experience of running charity shops who would like to work in ours. I had had plenty of experience in opening and running shops, but the processing and pricing of donated garments and other items was an area where I certainly needed someone with experience.

When I stopped to think, it was an enterprise totally new to me, and an interesting challenge to make it succeed. On the face of it, having all my saleable items donated and most of my staff working for free – and not paying any rates because I had persuaded Dudley Metropolitan Borough Council to rescind the 20 per cent rates levy which they were entitled to apply – it looked a pretty easy enterprise to move into profit! Quite a change from running the electrical store.

Some time previously, with the help of another board member, David Johnson, I had formed a separate trading company from the Hospice, which was to become VAT registered, passing over all its profits by deed of covenant to the Hospice at the end of each financial year, which was 31 March. The inaugural committee meeting of the Mary Stevens Hospice Trading Company was held on 17 February 1992, at the Hospice, with me as chairman and four other board members. Subsequent meetings were held at my home, Tinkers Cottage at Lawnswood.

To get the shop totally fitted out and painted, I had a loan of £10,000 from the main Hospice board, of which I was now a member, which I hoped to repay within the space of twelve months. I had small leaflets printed, explaining that a Hospice shop was to be opened in May, and asking for clean clothes, bric-a-brac, books and any other saleable items that would be collected within a few days. I had previously managed to get my old retired gardener, Tom Holland, to agree to distribute the leaflets around the Pedmore area and collect all the goods a few days later.

Once the shop was up and running, enough clothes became available every week without any need for leafleting. However, if people were unable to bring the garments into the shop and needed them collecting, this was where dear Tom came

The first Mary Stevens Hospice shop which Geoff opened in Victoria Passage, Stourbridge, 9 May 1992.

The official opening of the Brierley Hill Hospice shop by the Mayor of Dudley, Councillor Mary Whitehouse, accompanied by the Mayoress, Jean Richardson, with Geoff and Sue holding the ribbon, August 1993.

into his own. For years he religiously did all the collections for us several days a week, initially in his own car, later in the first small van that I bought. He had also helped me with painting the shop and staircase, which we did ourselves to help keep the cost down.

Nearer the opening date, I had the manageress and volunteers there to receive goods directly at the shop. People brought items in from far and wide, following my appeal on the local radio and in free newspapers. Finally, at 9 a.m. on Saturday 9 May 1992, our first Hospice shop was officially opened by the Mayor and Mayoress of Dudley. We were absolutely inundated with customers, taking £800 on the first day alone.

I had provisionally set myself a weekly target of £1,000, which, on my low expenditure base, I estimated would produce an annual profit of some £25,000. As well as producing an ongoing regular income for the Hospice, it also created a much-needed awareness that we wanted in those early days. We would actually have people coming into the shop asking, 'What's a hospice?' The volunteers would be able to explain or hand out details of the Hospice's facilities and of how it differed from their local hospitals. This was a procedure that would be followed as I opened other shops across the borough.

After only three months the bank balance was back to about the £10,000 mark, so I was able to repay the amount that I had borrowed from the main Hospice account. It was to be the first and last time that I needed financial help from the Hospice, as all my future shops and purchases would be funded by the Trading Company. I managed to find a fellow Stourbridge Rotarian, John Silcox, who agreed to pay the wages and compile the annual accounts, while I did the day-to-day handling of cash, paying of invoices and monitoring of bank accounts. At the end of the first twelve months I was able to hand over a massive £25,000, and this was after paying for all the opening expenses!

Twelve months later I was ready to embark on shop number two, going through the same procedure of looking round the local towns and checking out empty shops to find the most suitable premises. I finally settled on a double-fronted shop in Brierley Hill High Street, in a prominent position opposite the market. Once again, it was on two floors, but this time there was also a sizeable basement which could be approached from the rear, ideal for storing excess clothes and rags. 'Rags' is the term given to the clothes that are excluded from sale because they are soiled, worn, or otherwise not of the required standard. They are all bagged, together with clothes that still have not sold after being on display for a long period. These rags were collected once a week, and we received a cash payment for them that fluctuated over the years from nearly £3 per bag to less than £1 per bag. We could sometimes make up to forty or more bags per week from a shop. It was a very useful addition to the takings.

In the early days we did try one or two jumble sales at Hawbush Road Community Centre to get rid of excess clothes, but this involved so much extra work for a very small return that we decided just to rely on the 'rag man', as he was called. I did not need to advertise for a manageress for this second shop. The arrangement of having two manageresses sharing the role at the Stourbridge shop hadn't worked out too well; so one had had to go, leaving Pat Smith in charge five days per week, with a deputy to cover the other day and for holidays. Pat said that her daughter, Gail Radford, was very interested in the job of manageress at Brierley Hill; knowing Pat, I knew that she would not recommend her daughter unless she could handle the job. When I interviewed Gail, she straight away appeared the confident, friendly, energetic person that I was looking for.

This time the landlords were London-based, and it was with some difficulty that I managed to get the first year's rent reduced from £10,000 to £9,000, subsequently obtaining a six weeks' rent-free period on each of the first two years, thus saving another £2,300. They wanted to charge £750 legal fees, but I refused to pay more than £250 and eventually got my way. I was not a very easy person to negotiate with when working for a charity! Once again, the Mayor of Dudley opened the shop on 27 August 1993. Although it didn't take off as quickly as the Stourbridge one had done, I hadn't expected it to, as it was farther away from the Hospice and servicing a poorer area than Stourbridge.

About this time I was asked to advise Kemp Hospice at Kidderminster about opening their first hospice shop, and this I was more than happy to do.

By the end of March 1994 the profit from the two shops had shot up to £60,000. It was about this time that, in talking to the estate agent John Widdowson, who was the letting agent for the Stourbridge shop, I found out that the upstairs of shop

Geoff with a party of Stourbridge Hospice shop volunteers at a Hospice 'thank you' evening.

premises are often not used. As the shop next door was empty, I made a deal that enabled us to take over the whole of the upstairs, which would be increased in size by the landlord removing the staircase, filling in the cavity, and knocking through a good-sized section of the wall that separated it from the upstairs of our shop. He agreed to do this for a minimal increase in rent of only £750 per year. At the same time, I arranged to have free use of the downstairs, as our occupancy saved the landlord paying the proportion of council tax that would be due on the empty property.

I was ecstatic. I had doubled the size of the shop for less than £15 per week! This arrangement was to last for several years, but, as other empty premises in Victoria Passage became let, I was afraid that the one of which I had free use would also be let, so I negotiated a vastly reduced rental of only £1,500 per year and took over both shops on a permanent basis. I was able to get the landlord to open up an entrance between the two shops on the ground floor, similar to the one he had made upstairs.

I remember both Brierley Hill and Stourbridge shops putting on fashion shows in those early years to raise a few hundred pounds. The models were the volunteers, and they kept back some beautiful outfits which later sold for the princely sums of £10 to £15. These events were lots of fun and provided a bit more publicity for the Hospice shops. Incidentally, it took two years before we got a full complement of reliable volunteers at Brierley Hill. One day Sue went over to Brierley Hill market opposite the shop, to enquire if they knew of anyone who could help us for a few hours a week. They listened carefully, but when they knew that they wouldn't be paid, the sharp response was, 'We don't do owt for now't 'ere, lass!'

Early in the Trading Company years, I had seen a need to thank volunteers for giving their time and dedication so willingly every week for the benefit of the Hospice. The first year, just before Christmas, when there was only the Stourbridge shop, Sue and I were able to invite them all round to our house to give them drinks and bites to eat. I remember it being a lovely evening because a small choir of carol singers that I knew happened to come round that evening and we were able to invite them in to sing for us. In future years, when there were just too many to accommodate at home, I arranged for a 'thank you' evening to be held at the Hospice during the summer months so that we could sit outside if possible. If the matron was available I would ask her to say a few words of thanks before adding my own, telling of any news on future shops or of anything else that would be of interest. They were lovely nights and appreciated by all our wonderful volunteers.

In about May 1997, our paid fundraiser, Gerald Wood, who had been made a member of the Trading Company, said that he had found premises suitable for our next Hospice shop at Cradley Heath. I went over next day to inspect it and found it quite a distance removed from the busy shopping area and far too small, as we were then moving into selling furniture. While in Cradley Heath, I thought I would have a good look around myself, and found a large, empty showroom with rear access and parking, in a fine position and absolutely ideal for our requirements. The only downside was that it was totally boarded up; therefore, on first appearances it was quite intimidating. I enquired at neighbouring shops and found that it had been vandalised internally and had been empty for some two years.

It may sound crazy to you, but this was just the sort of news I wanted to hear, because I knew the landlord would be desperate by now to get a tenant in. Negotiations over the rental were long and hard, but I was in no hurry, and the agent assured me that there was no competition on the horizon. In the end, some six months later I settled for a five-year lease at £7,500, commencing with a six months' rent-free period which saved £3,750 – far more than it cost me to have laminated cladding fitted around the walls. With this done and a lick of paint everywhere, it soon looked like a brand new shop. I was later to find out that the market rental price for a shop of this size and in this position was some £20,000! Gail Radford, who had opened the Brierley Hill shop for me and had subsequently left to take up a post at Rackhams, had suddenly lost her post there. She was delighted to open the third Hospice shop for me, with the official opening being carried out on this occasion by the Mayor of Sandwell. The date was Friday 9 January 1998.

When interviewing staff for either van-driving or managing the shop, I always explained that it was never going to be a highly paid job because maximum profit must go to the Hospice; I also stated that I would quite understand if they had mortgages to pay and needed more than I was offering. Van drivers and deputy managers were only started on a minimum-wage basis, while managers received rather more. Not only were costs being kept to an absolute minimum, I was also getting staff who were not doing it solely for the money, but because they wanted to be involved in helping a worthy cause.

With the extensions to the Stourbridge shop, and having large premises at Cradley Heath, the small van that I had originally purchased was proving inadequate

*Hospice shop in
High Street,
Cradley Heath,
1997.*

for the large amount of furniture we were selling. Over the next few years I was able to supply from the Geoff Hill store two second-hand Ford Transit vans with a high dome and long wheelbase, which were ideal for the job. When more shops came on the scene I also bought another smaller van out of my charitable trust.

Later in 1998 we were offered the opportunity of taking over the lease of a Cancer Research shop in Stone Street, Dudley. The premises were on two floors with rather more space on the upper floor, the disadvantage being that it was not in a dynamic shopping area and customers had to be 'attracted' to walk the extra 50yd or so off Dudley High Street. The manageress had agreed to stay on, and to encourage her volunteers to stay also. Initial indications were that she had been taking the £1,000 per week I was looking for, but events certainly did not work out that way, as average takings for the first three months were only £558, not much above a break-even figure. The shop was actually owned by Dudley Metropolitan Borough Council and had a rental of £8,000 per annum which we eventually got reduced to £6,500.

Sue and I were not impressed with how it was being run and found clothes had been put on display that were quite obviously soiled, and that there was an untidy pile of bin-bagged garments always stacked outside the workroom. Unfortunately, there was no other solution but to replace the manageress. As soon as new blood was introduced the takings improved to an acceptable level.

When I opened the first Hospice shop at Stourbridge, I realised that I also needed to sell birthday cards and gift-wrap. I found a large, privately owned warehouse at Blackheath carrying good stock that would give me an appreciable discount off trade prices for all purchases. The owner happened to be a long-time customer of mine, which helped, and I was to go there every two months or so for the next ten years to top up on stock. Soon I was carrying over thirty different 'relation' cards as well as the sympathy, get well, anniversary, thank you and blanks. I could buy lovely cards in boxes of 144, which usually included twelve different designs and cost only 10p per card. I can tell you, they really flew out at 40p each, particularly in the Stourbridge shop, and quite well at the Hospice too. The gift-wrap was really super quality and, once again, cost only 10p per sheet, to sell at 25p in the early years.

Not content with the cards and gift-wrap, I soon wanted to extend the 'bought in' goods range. Sue and I would go to the 'market trader' types of warehouse at Bilston, Willenhall and Walsall, where all the goods were so cheap you could put well over 100 per cent mark-up on them and they were still a bargain price. We would buy in ornaments, picture frames, gardening gloves and tools, artists' oil and watercolour paints, brushes, notebooks, teddy bears; and literally anything else that took our eye. As well as taking a whole day sourcing the many boxes of goods, it took another day spent at home to unwrap and price everything up. It was practically all made in China and so, unbelievably cheap. For instance, a whole box containing twelve tubes of oil or watercolour paints would cost only 65p. I would buy these ten dozen boxes at a time and sell them at £1.95. They were quite good quality, and the art students at Stourbridge College would buy several boxes at a time when I had them in stock.

After two or three years of buying Christmas cards from EMS, their representative, who called round to our house every year with samples, decided to leave and set up on a freelance basis. He soon had contact with some of the top birthday card and gift-wrap manufacturers – Medici, Caspari and others – and was able to offer me end-of-line merchandise of superb quality at absolute giveaway prices. For six or seven years he had been regularly driving up from Bristol with samples, and I was able to introduce him to Gail Radford before Sue and I decided to retire from Hospice fundraising.

On Thursday 14 August 1999, the Millennium Mayor of Dudley, Councillor Fred Hunt, and the Mayoress opened our fifth Hospice shop. It was right at the end of the row of shops in Lower Gornal and was, once again, on two floors, although on this occasion there were enough rooms downstairs to allocate one as a workroom, leaving all the upstairs available for storage. I had known the landlord many years before and we agreed a rental of £3,500, with a rent-free period of two months to help us get off the ground. When the lease was finally agreed I was on a very tight schedule to open, as on the following day Sue and I had booked a flight to see my daughter Teresa and the five grandchildren in America. There was a lot of remedial work to be done in a very short space of time, but I had a good carpenter and plumber, and Gerald had said that Tom, one of our staff at the Hospice, was a professional painter and would be able to do the paintwork. It was only when he came to do the painting, just over a week before opening, that I found he could only come for two days. Panic bells were ringing, but a fellow Stourbridge Rotarian came to my assistance and sent two men along. The paint was just about dry when the Mayor arrived! Even on Saturday and Sunday Gail and a volunteer friend were working there, processing clothes in order to get everything ready for the big day.

I always found Gornal to be more of a community-based area than some of the other towns where I had opened shops. Volunteers for the Hospice shop were much easier to find than in places like Brierley Hill, Cradley Heath, Dudley and even

Geoff's fifth Hospice shop was opened at Lower Gornal by the Millennium Mayor of Dudley, Councillor Fred Hunt, accompanied by his wife, the Mayoress, August 1999.

Halesowen. The relief manageress that I had at Stourbridge for many years took over the post at Gornal and soon settled into the job, making another sizeable and regular weekly contribution to the Hospice running costs.

Later in the year 2000 I was approached by a man I knew at Stourbridge to see if I would be interested in taking over a shop in Halesowen, which they were running for a church charity and were having problems with. It was situated in a secondary position alongside two other charity shops but, as the lease expired in October 2001, it seemed a chance to give it a good shot for a few months to see if there was future potential in the premises. It was nice, modern premises on two floors with a wide-open staircase, so that the upper floor could be used for sales display as well as a workroom. The rental was £8,000, which was roughly what I was prepared to pay for premises there; when I had an independent survey carried out I was told that £9,000 to £9,500 would be appropriate.

Incidentally, all the Hospice shops are on what is known as 'full repairing leases'. It is therefore imperative to have a structural survey carried out before taking on a lease in order that any deficiencies in the property are noted. We would then not be held responsible for rectifying them when the lease was finally terminated. I usually asked my solicitor and friend, Bob Farrow at Stephensons, Brierley Hill, to recommend a surveyor, and on this occasion he recommended one at Stourport. I phoned him and asked how soon he could do it and what it would cost. 'I can do it some time next week and let you have a full schedule a few days later. The cost will

Geoff's sixth and last Hospice shop was opened at Halesowen by the Mayor of Dudley, Councillor George Davies and his wife, the Mayoress, in 2000. Also present were Irene Layton of the Halesowen fundraising group and Linda O'Brian, manageress.

be £300,' he said. I then talked on for some time about it being to raise money for a local hospice and that we were desperate for any help he could give by reducing the price. It went quiet for a while and then he said, 'You win, OK, I'll only charge you half price, £150'. 'Well,' I said, 'if that's the best you can do I suppose we'll have to accept it!' I somehow had the natural aptitude to drive a hard bargain for the Hospice on every possible occasion, that I never had all the years in my own business! I was later to find out that, over the years, my solicitor never charged for his time in all his dealings with the shops. I think he respected the time and effort that I had put in as a local businessman, and he said that this was his way of making a contribution to the Hospice. He had certainly done it in a very unassuming and appreciated manner.

During the weeks that I was looking at and negotiating the Halesowen shop, I had a much younger volunteer than usual working at Stourbridge. Her name was Linda O'Brien. Linda was a bubbly, energetic and very self-motivated person, just the type to open a charity shop in a new area. When I suggested her being manageress at Halesowen she jumped at the chance and worked hard to get it opened by Friday 9 February 2001. The official opening was carried out by the Mayor and Mayoress of Dudley, Councillor and Mrs George Davies.

A Birmingham-based property speculator, whom I had met several times and came to know quite well, owned the shop. I don't think he knew too much about hospices because, although I showed him a current balance sheet and told him of the track record of the Hospice Trading Company, he still wanted me to sign a personal indemnity that I would pay the rent for the duration of the lease if 'anything went wrong'. Actually, I didn't make a big deal of it, knowing how sound the company was, and – I think to his surprise – signed it immediately.

The shop took off well, joining Cradley Heath, Brierley Hill and Gornal with takings of about £1,000 per week, with Dudley, now much better under new management, not far behind. Stourbridge had settled down with weekly takings around the £2,000 mark. It meant that at the end of March 2001, I was able to hand over £120,000 to the Hospice.

I went to the Halesowen shop most weeks, and saw how attractive and smart it was always kept. It is never easy to run a fairly large shop on two floors, often with only one volunteer there. Later that year Linda left. It was only when a replacement manageress came on the scene and takings started a downward slide that we appreciated her worth. Eventually a new manageress was found, although volunteers remained in short supply.

At the end of March 2002, after what eventually turned out to be my last full year of running the Hospice shops, the profit was up for the tenth successive year to an appreciable £140,000!

On 9 May 2002, the 10th anniversary of my opening of the first Hospice shop at Victoria Passage, Stourbridge, I realised that a lot of the volunteers who were still turning up to help every week were part of the thirty-five I had recruited all those years ago. I asked Pat Smith, the manageress, who was also still there, to make a list of the 'ten year brigade', as I would like to take them out for a meal to celebrate and thank them for their continued dedication over this long period of time. At first it seemed that one or two didn't want to come if it meant that Hospice money was to be spent on the meals, as they really valued all Hospice money that much. It was only when Pat explained that I would be treating them that their names went on the list, and I was amazed to find that a total of eighteen were still there after ten years. Sadly, three or four had died, and others had had to leave owing to poor health or because they had moved out of the area, but hardly anyone else had stopped.

I always said, when I was giving a talk about the Hospice, that in a way the shops were an 'all win' operation. The people who donated clothes and goods that they no longer wanted felt good about it because they were going to help a local cause. The volunteers certainly enjoyed their day or half-day at the shop, working in a friendly and worthwhile environment. The people who made purchases from it were mostly not very well off and appreciated buying a bargain. Last, but not least, a great deal of money was made on a regular basis that went towards the ever-increasing costs of running the Hospice.

Getting back to the volunteers, Sue and I eventually took them all out to Luciano's Restaurant, just a few doors away from the Hospice shop. We all had a super time together, and I was able to thank them all personally for the very important part they had played in making our flagship premises so successful.

A few weeks later, we had our last 'thank you' evening at the Hospice for volunteers from all the shops. It was tinged with sadness because, by then, they knew that I would be finishing my fundraising sojourn at the Hospice, and none of them wanted me to leave. I was able to tell the eighty or so there that, through their efforts over the last ten years, the unbelievable total of £1 million had been raised.

16

The Mary Stevens Hospice Lottery

During 1995 it became apparent that one or two hospices, mainly in the north of the country, were running their own weekly lottery that was proving to be a good money-spinner. It had originated when Eileen Hanson set up a company, Starvale Management Ltd, who had their own computer programme and, for a percentage of the profits, would help start a lottery at any hospice.

The first hospice lottery in the country was at St Catherine's Hospice, Preston: proving very successful, lottery fundraising was now being taken up by many others. We applied to Starvale for more information, only to be told that Compton Hospice had just registered most of the Dudley borough as their territory, leaving us virtually only Stourbridge and Stourton to operate in. This would have made it totally impossible to run and the only alternative was to start our own lottery: but where could we obtain the know-how to operate one?

We eventually found that a large hospice, St Anne's at Manchester, had been running their own lottery for eighteen months or so. Mr William Stuart, who was the appeals coordinator there, kindly offered to talk us through the procedure if we wished to go along to their offices. Our fundraiser Gerald Wood, I, and four other members of the board, drove to Manchester, to spend 3 to 4 hours with William going through the ramifications and possible pitfalls of running a lottery. Towards the end of our visit I had a quiet word with William, asking him if he could convince our board members that we needed to go ahead with our lottery, especially if we were to get a residential facility off the ground. Not only did he speak to them there, but also he kindly arranged to come to our Hospice in order to address a full board meeting in February 1996.

I was away on holiday and unable to attend this board meeting, but I submitted my usual Trading Company Report, adding that I thought it imperative to start a lottery. I also recommended that a start be made to adding a much-needed Residential Unit to our Day Care Centre. This was something that I thought we greatly needed to move forward, as the Trading Company was now providing a large part of the money required to run the Day Hospice.

At the board meeting it was agreed the time had come to launch our own lottery. The board decided that they wanted Gerald to concentrate on all other forms of fundraising; therefore I agreed to form a separate Lottery Company and be both its chairman and promoter.

Not long afterwards, Bryan Marshall and I went up to Manchester for a further discussion with William Stuart. He had commenced the Manchester Hospice Lottery with a weekly prize fund of £3,000 and suggested that I do the same; however, talking it through further with him I found that it was several months into the draw before they reached a break-even point. Therefore, I decided to pitch the initial prize fund at £2,000, hoping to recruit some 3,000 players in the first three months, during which time we were allowed to canvass before the first draw took place. After the first thirty weeks I increased the prize fund to £3,000. Needing an attractive first prize, I decided that it should be set at £1,000, and I also made certain there would be lots of other winners by having five prizes of £100, ten of £50 and a hundred of £10, making, in all, 116 prizes every week. I was able to implement this prize structure from week thirty onwards.

I felt that it would probably be much easier for collectors to pay into local post offices rather than fight their way through to town-centre banks. Therefore, I opened an account at the Co-operative Bank's Wolverhampton Branch, as they had an arrangement for receiving cash paid in at post offices. I spoke at some length with the branch manager, who eventually agreed to grant us free banking. I was exceedingly pleased to get this support because I could envisage, even at this early stage, that there would be a large number of small transactions involving a considerable amount of cash – which banks are never happy about because of the time it takes to count and the weight to transport it. I was also hoping to have a lot of players signed up on small-value standing orders, which, once again, would be expensive for them to monitor. On the credit side I was able to offer him a sizeable build-up of the cash profit from the lottery over a twelve months' period. As with the trading company, money would only be passed over to the main Hospice account on an annual basis.

When starting the Lottery in March 1996, I borrowed £10,000 from the main Hospice account. Manchester Hospice had suggested I would need £20,000 to £25,000, but I thought that if I could get money coming in straight away I could manage with much less. Bryan Marshall and I interviewed the rather small number of applicants who replied to my advertisement for a computer operator/lottery manager, and for a field manager to organise collectors and canvassers. Unsurprisingly, no one had any experience of running a lottery, so the learning curve was going to be very steep for all of us. We eventually settled on a computer operator, and also chose Tony Raffan for the very difficult and responsible job of recruiting canvassers and collectors. There were only thirteen weeks left before our first draw. As well as building up 'rounds' for the collectors to gather the £2 fortnightly payments, we also had many people whom we encouraged to pay by a standing order of £13, £26 or £52. Finally, before the thirteen weeks were completed, I had what we called 'single tickets', which we sold at the Hospice shops and any other outlet that Tony or I could find.

Jeff Jephcott, editor of the News Group Stourbridge, Halesowen and Dudley weekly free newspapers, gave us plenty of publicity. I asked him if it would be

Keith Skelding of Stourbridge, the Hospice's first lottery winner, with Uta Pritchards, lottery manager, and Geoff, July 1996.

possible for us to publish a full weekly list of winners from our Friday draw. He said he was not too happy about publishing results nearly a week late, as the newspapers would be delivered only on the following Thursday. He asked me if I could get the time of the computerised draw changed from Friday to early Wednesday morning, making sure that the winners' names were faxed to him by 10 a.m. This was a brilliant idea, because the public would then see all the results in print the following day.

It took a little reorganisation to get all the payments in and recorded by Tuesday afternoon, but somehow we managed to do it. Abbreviated results of all the main weekly prize-winners were printed in the three local *Chronicle* newspapers as well. This was a tremendous saving in both cost and time; most other lotteries had to get result sheets printed, for the collectors to distribute the following week as they called for their collections.

As 10 July 1996, the date of the first draw, approached, I could see that it was going to be touch and go whether we would manage to reach our target of 3,000 players. Eventually we had 3,160 in the first draw, a great achievement for all involved and a reward for their hard work and commitment. We were in profit straight away.

It became even better afterwards, as we hit the 4,000 barrier in week five, 5,000 in week nine, and 6,000 in week thirteen. In the Christmas-week draw at the end of 1996 we just managed to reach 7,000, and were by then making really substantial profits for the Hospice. By the end of March 1997, we were able to hand over from the shops and lottery the massive sum of £170,000 – exactly twice as much as the previous year's £85,000, which had been from the shops only. After allowing for support received from the local health authority, the total costs for running the Day

Hospice were only some £120,000. This meant that for the financial year ending March 1997, a surplus of £50,000, plus all the fundraising from trusts, legacies and the local community, could be allocated towards the projected new residential facility.

I must tell you a little story about Flo, Sue's mother, who was aged about 85 when I started the lottery and had decided to pay for five goes every week: one for herself and four for members of her family. This amounted to £65 for the quarter and she wrote out her cheque accordingly. Some ten weeks or so later she received her reminder for the next quarter's cheque, which had to be received and cleared in time for the appropriate draw. So another £65 was sent off. Three months later the same thing happened again and Flo, who is an old-time businesswoman and does not throw money away lightly, said to Sue, 'You know I've paid for five goes every week all this time and haven't even had a £10 win in this lottery! Geoff's the promoter isn't he? Surely he can do something about it for me!' Unfortunately Geoff couldn't do anything about it for dear Flo because the draw itself was all computerised. However, it all ended happily a few weeks later, when her granddaughter won the top prize of £1,000, which solved Flo's problem and mine!

Although the lottery was profitable in the early stages, it was certainly not devoid of problems. The lady whom I had employed as computer operator had unfortunately not come up to expectations and had to be replaced in October by a member of the Hospice staff, Mrs Jane Jukes, who was assisted by a very helpful team of part-time volunteers. Then in December I received a long resignation letter from Tony Raffan, our field manager – the last thing that I needed just before Christmas. I felt that he had tried his utmost to carry out a very difficult job. All credit to him, we now had nearly 7,000 members on board and he had certainly set us off on the right track.

The main problem was always going to be reliable collectors. We usually worked with about sixty or seventy and although most were reliable, if any let us down at short notice (and many did), it became the field manager's task to find a replacement, and failing that, to do it himself. The alternative would be to lose several hundred pounds and upset many people because they would be excluded from the draw for the next two weeks.

Early in 1997 it was decided by a number of promoters that it might be helpful to have a national meeting so that we could discuss our problems and, hopefully, learn a few things from each other – as hospice fundraisers and shop representatives had been doing for some years. Bill Clark, lottery promoter at Willen Hospice, Milton Keynes, offered to host the inaugural meeting, with representatives of nineteen hospices from all over the country attending. Even two ladies from Ayr Hospice in Scotland made the trip!

The meeting was held on 27 February 1997. After initial introductions Ruth Gardiner, from Ayr Hospice, gave her presentation on the very successful lottery they had running in Scotland. Later, I gave a presentation on how we presently stood with our lottery, being in operation less than eight months and by then having 7,286 players. The rest of the morning and the afternoon sessions were spent in open discussion, with group meetings on the various aspects of promoting and running a lottery. The whole day was very informative, particularly for a few representatives present who were starting or contemplating beginning their own lottery. The day concluded with a tour of the hospice, which was beautifully situated on the edge of a huge lake.

Under lottery rules the prize fund has to be more than 25 per cent of the weekly takings, so early in 1997 I took the decision to increase the weekly prizes to £3,000. It was also about this time that total takings exceeded £100,000 and the lottery passed out of the jurisdiction of the local authority, to come under the control of the Gaming Board of Great Britain, with a much closer monitoring of our activities. Every week a four-page profit and loss form had to be completed, with items of expenditure allocated over a proportionate number of weeks, so that the final figure of weekly profit represented, as far as possible, a true figure for that particular week. At the end of the financial year the totals in the annual accounts should correspond to the total of the fifty-two weekly returns.

On 7 October 1997 we staged the second National Lottery Seminar at Mary Stevens Hospice in our new meeting room. We had a similar number of hospices represented and at the end of a very full day everyone agreed that the exchange of ideas had made it all well worthwhile. This was followed by a further meeting held at Mary Stevens Hospice on 24 March 1998. I think that being in the centre of the country made us ideally situated for representatives travelling from London and the south, as well as the north of England, with one person still coming from Ayr in Scotland.

Our ticket outlets now numbered fifty. The 'A' boards, which were needed outside the shops, proved quite expensive to buy. A carpenter I happened to know had helped in the past at the Old Park Special Needs School, Holly Hall, Dudley, and offered to get the students there to make a supply of them. They very kindly did this free of charge and thoroughly enjoyed the experience of making something useful and practical.

On 27 October 1998 we held our fourth national meeting at the Hospice and, out of the seventeen represented, we came third, behind Ayr and Manchester, in numbers of lottery members. We all agreed that this was very satisfying and represented all the hard work that everyone had put into achieving the 8,400 players we had by then.

It was late in 1998 that I was to attend one of our Trading Company regional meetings at the Shrewsbury

Left to right: Schoolmaster Bill Rex, with pupils Harry Matthews, Mohbeen Aktow, Martyn Plant and Michaela Cole, and Geoff.

Sue and Geoff at a Hospice fête stall promoting the Hospice lottery, 1998.

Hospice, where I had to park around the back and enter through a side door. I hadn't a clue which way to go in this rather large residential hospice and asked the first person I saw if he would kindly point me in the right direction for our meeting room. 'Sure,' he said, 'I'm going that way. It's a bit complicated so I'll show you.' 'That's very kind of you,' I replied, and by way of making conversation added, 'What's your position at the hospice?' 'I'm lottery promoter,' he replied. 'What a coincidence,' I said, 'because I also happen to be the lottery chairman and promoter of ours.' At first he was quite taken aback by my potential workload, but was very keen to have a good chat about our lottery experiences. 'Would you mind if we met up at lunchtime to have a chat and exchange ideas?' he asked 'Not at all,' I replied, 'that would suit me fine.' He came at 1 p.m. when we broke for lunch and, instead of talking about shops, I was suddenly talking about lotteries!

I mention all this because, as a result of our conversation that day, a valuable piece of information came my way when he said, 'By the way, Geoff, we've just started a trial run on telesales to promote our lottery.' This was certainly something new and exciting and I asked how it was progressing. He said that they were getting quite a good response and that it was costing about £7 to £10 per new member. This sounded quite a lot, but if that person stayed in the lottery for only a year they would pay £52. A vast potential for profit was unfolding as we spoke.

Arriving back home, I looked through the list of members of the Black Country Chamber of Commerce and found a local telesales organisation, and managed to persuade them to do a trial run of 1,000 calls at 50p per phone call: we were in business. Experience soon revealed that if people did not register to join the lottery immediately, then a second phone call was necessary about ten or so days later, following the despatch of details.

We had reasonably good results from this company for about twelve months, and then one night I was invited to Dudley and District Business Club to give a talk about the Hospice. In conversation after the meeting, hoping to gain a few new members, I was approached by a lady who said, 'My name is Judy Owen, I run a team of telesales girls and would like to help you with your lottery.' This sounded ideal. Judy had been running her business from home for some years but was about to move into commercial premises. There were two spare lines at her house and she didn't mind having two telesales girls there at night carrying out calls on behalf of the Hospice: furthermore, she seemed a very keen and efficient young lady. I took up her offer and she personally monitored the girls, seeing that the results were faxed through to the lottery office on a daily basis so that they could be attended to immediately.

After a few years of operating the lottery, we were finding that some thirty or so players were being lost each week for a variety of reasons, meaning that we had to get thirty more on board just to stand still. Over the next few years, telesales helped tremendously to increase the number playing in the lottery. Judy's help continued until 2001. By then we had room for our own telesales team in the new lottery office, so we instituted an in-house operation from then onwards.

Once the telesales operation was in full swing and proving successful at recruiting new players, I began to wonder if we could do more to prevent people from dropping out of our lottery by contacting them by telephone. I knew the lottery staff and volunteers did their best with the limited time they had available, but wondered if a couple of hours spent one night a week would be a worthwhile and cost-effective way of retaining some of these people in our lottery. The simple way to find out, so I thought, was to ask my dear wife, Sue, to have a go for a couple of hours and see how it went. Although I say it myself, and of course may be biased, Sue has a very good telephone manner and, more importantly, knew much about the Hospice itself – just in case, as often did happen, questions were asked about other aspects of its work. Sue not only did a test run very successfully, but every Monday evening from 6 p.m. until 8 p.m. she would phone people who had not renewed on their cheque payments. This went on for some two years, during which time she encouraged many hundreds of people to rejoin our lottery, a large number of them by taking out standing orders, which was extremely profitable from the Hospice's point of view.

I had had one or two tussles over the years with the Co-operative Bank regarding the free banking facility negotiated when I first started the lottery. It seemed that each time there was a change of management, someone would ring up to say that they could not possibly carry on giving a totally free service because of the vast number of transactions being carried out each week. I would reciprocate by pleading poverty and negotiate a little more free time. The last person rang late in the year 2000, when there were some 9,000-odd weekly players, being quite emphatic that a charge would have to be made and suggesting it would be in the order of £5,500 per annum. To give me a bit of breathing space I said that I could not sanction this payment without consultation with the lottery treasurer and would phone this person back.

In actual fact I phoned the lottery manager at St Anne's Hospice, Manchester. My thinking was that the Co-operative Bank was based at Manchester, and I figured that it would not be good publicity for them if it got into the local papers that they were charging their local Hospice such a vast amount of money. I explained to him how much the bank was proposing to charge and waited for a reaction. I didn't have to wait long. He was absolutely astounded, continuing by saying that they had never been approached by the Co-operative Bank for payments, also that their lottery had been running a couple of years longer than ours and had many more members.

Needless to say, I was soon on the phone to the bank and speaking to the person who had 'laid it on the line', telling of the conversation that I had just had with the Manchester-based hospice. The person said that she would speak to her superiors. I never had a problem with the bank after that.

Being a businessman myself I could see where the bank was coming from, but I would like to add how grateful we were to the Co-operative Bank for the very kind help and support they gave over the years.

It was probably from the beginning of 1999 that the lottery started to see the benefit of the excellent staff at its helm. Jenny Hemmings, with Debby Haynes who had been with the lottery for twelve months, had together become an extremely capable partnership. They were later joined by Rosalie Rider, who helped part time. Added to this were also our very experienced and dedicated volunteers: suddenly the lottery seemed to run like clockwork. The monthly meetings of the early years were suddenly a thing of the past. Later, when Sue Roden became field manager, supervising the collectors and canvassers, even that most challenging aspect of operating the lottery seemed to be running into smooth waters. Throughout my business life I have often said that you are only as good as your staff and this certainly now proved the case with the lottery.

I remember going into the Lottery office one morning and saying to Jenny and Debbie in a mock stern voice, 'Do you know I'm getting fed up with you two?' 'Why? What's the matter, Geoff?' was the shocked reply. 'Because I'm the trouble-shooter for the Lottery and since you've come on the scene there's no trouble to shoot and you're making me redundant!' I exclaimed. They just laughed with relief and got straight back to their work, which was typical of them. A mention must also be made of John Clarke; although a very quietly spoken person and a non-driver, he managed for several years to canvass very successfully for the lottery, and also sold our single tickets in vast numbers at Hospice fêtes and other fundraising functions.

On several occasions I had complaints from loyal lottery players of ours, that Compton Hospice had been round canvassing or leafleting their area to induce them to join their Wolverhampton-based lottery. These were people who lived Stourbridge side of Brierley Hill and Kingswinford; I therefore thought it time to have a serious discussion with Compton Hospice about it, and arranged a morning meeting with their chief executive and lottery manager at our Hospice.

The chief executive seemed genuinely surprised when I told him that our catchment area was effectively only the 300,000 people in the Dudley borough in which they also ran their shops in Dudley and Brierley Hill. On the other hand their catchment area encompassed five times the number of inhabitants and in addition

Left to right: Maggie Hutchinson, Laura Twells, Debbie Haynes, Irene Colgan and Dawn Scott, lottery office staff, celebrating with Geoff in raising £250,000, 2001.

had funding from five different area health authorities. Although they both listened patiently to my request to kindly leave the adjacent territory solely to us, a few weeks later I had a further complaint. When I again rang the chief executive, he just intimated that they had to raise over £3 million per year to run Compton Hospice, and as they still took some patients from Dudley borough he was still going ahead with the campaign. I did suggest that as they invariably had a waiting list for Compton Hospice and that we often had beds to spare, it might be a good idea if we took all the patients from the Dudley borough. It went quiet for a second or two, then he said that would not be his decision to make but one for the medical team. I did report this conversation to our Hospice board but never heard anything further. I might add that at the time of their visit we had over 11,000 players in our lottery, while Compton were still struggling with roughly 8,000 or so.

I personally helped Compton Hospice quite a lot over the years and had got to know their matron of over twenty years, Ross Kensey, quite well in the process. When they opened their new day unit in Sandwell I decided to donate all the electrical appliances that they required. Ross was very appreciative and invited Sue and me over for a personally conducted tour of the facility when it was opened.

When Ross eventually retired from Compton Hospice, her husband invited Sue and me to a surprise 'This is Your Life' that was staged for her in a Wolverhampton club one evening. It was a wonderful experience for Ross, as friends and colleagues from over the years appeared on stage in turn to recount memorable tales about this remarkable lady. Unfortunately, when the compère announced how she had helped to get the Mary Stevens Hospice new day centre up and running and that their secretary was here to tell us all about it, a sudden silence descended upon the packed hall. I immediately sensed that there was some mishap and stood up in the audience to explain, as a board member of the Hospice, how appreciative we were to have someone of Ross's experience to guide us through our successful opening period. I know that Ross and her husband were very glad of my quick thinking on this occasion, as the whole event was being filmed and there would otherwise have been a horrible gap in the proceedings.

Our lottery was by now raising huge sums of money. In the financial year ending 31 March 2001 it raised what I then thought an amazing amount of £230,000, which, together with the £120,000 from the shops, made a grand total of £350,000. I thought at the time that this was a vast amount; but twelve months later I was able to hand over to the main Hospice account £305,000 from the lottery and £140,000 from the shops, a grand total of £445,000. This was an increase of £95,000 in only twelve months. I was also able to inform the lottery staff, volunteers and the main Hospice board that, as well as the Trading Company raising a total of £1 million, the Lottery Company had also hit this magic figure – and in only six years!

It was unbelievable that projects started from nothing could raise over £2 million in just ten years and, once set up, would go on contributing £500,000 or so on an annual basis towards the running costs of the Hospice – unlike general fundraising events which are a one-off, and can be very much hit and miss.

Back row, left to right: Gerald Wood (fundraiser), Paul Lippitt (field manager), Geoff Hill (promoter) with, front row: Debbie Haynes, Jenny Hemming, Sue Roden (retiring field manager) and Rosalie Rider.

17

The Mary Stevens Hospice Main Board

I had only been fundraising for just over a year when, on 12 June 1992, I was invited to be a member of the main Hospice board. I didn't need a second invitation! I instantly found them to be a lovely group of people, all with their 'hearts in the right place', determined to get the Hospice off the ground and financially viable as quickly as possible.

One or two I already knew, such as Jim Higgs, an old friend from my school days and now a retired regional bank manager, and Mrs Phill Tilley, a physiotherapist who treated patients at the Hospice on a voluntary basis. They were joined by our secretary, Jock Poyner, an ex-Mayor of Dudley; David Johnson, an accountant; a very astute treasurer, Frank Rawcliffe; and three other local councillors who were co-opted onto the board. Our sister-in-charge, Miss Sara Hiam, handled the medical side, and our very capable chairman was local businessman, Bryan Marshall.

Board meetings were held regularly at about two-monthly intervals, and usually lasted for anything up to three hours, occasionally even longer. Until the Hospice was up and running, Ross Kensey, matron of Compton Hospice, Wolverhampton, attended to help and advise on our way forward.

We were licensed to take fifteen day patients for five days per week. The cost of this was initially some £200,000 per year, later rising to £250,000; 50 per cent of this was to be funded by the local health authority. It was on the long-awaited opening day and late in the morning (so the story went), that the odd-job man was summoned to the sister-in-charge, given a few pounds and told to fetch a small bottle of brandy. A second story went round later, explaining that it had been for a patient's consumption and not for the sister-in-charge! We soon started getting very good feedback from the initial intake of patients, with the bathing facilities being particularly beneficial for people who were elderly or physically impaired.

Once the Hospice was up and running and financially viable, our thoughts focused on having a dignitary for the 'Official Opening' to give it much-needed publicity, which would help tremendously, in those early days, with the fundraising. After a few delays and disappointments we were fortunate enough to be able to have HRH the Princess of Wales accept our invitation, with the date of 5 March 1992 firmly set for her to carry out this function.

Princess Diana talking to the Compton Hospice matron, Ross Kensey, at the official opening of the Mary Stevens Hospice Day Unit, 5 March 1992.

As the day approached it was 'all systems go' to make it as memorable a day as possible, and that's exactly what it turned out to be. On the right-hand side of the drive, up to the entrance, a large, open-fronted marquee was erected for all the invited volunteers from the shops, Hospice and fundraising groups to attend. To the right-hand side of the Hospice entrance was a small parking area, where I had arranged for one of the school bands to sit and entertain the crowds while waiting for Princess Diana to arrive. On the left-hand side of the drive and down to the main road stood the general public, who came in droves to see our magical Princess. She arrived with her police entourage and our chairman showed her round the Hospice, introducing her to patients who were attending on that day. She was absolutely lovely with everyone, and certainly gave them all her time.

I was positioned in the bathing area to show the Princess our facilities; my wife, Sue, who had been practising her curtsey and formal address, was with me. When the Princess came into the room with extended hand and a big, disarming smile, Sue just shook her hand, smiled back and said 'Hello!' The Princess was so natural that any formality would have seemed inappropriate. After the Hospice tour was completed, she not only went to the crowd assembled outside, but also continued right around into Hagley Road, accepting flowers and shaking hands. The crowds were ecstatic and the Hospice had some wonderful publicity from the occasion.

The years rolled by and everything went reasonably smoothly, but there were times when I felt that the board was lacking in medical direction. This was

Princess Diana meeting the crowds after the official opening of the Hospice in March 1992.

rectified in January 1995, when Miss Jean Faulkner, an ex-matron of St Mary's Hospice, a large residential and day hospice in Birmingham, joined us on the Hospice board.

Extensions were carried out to the lodge adjoining the Day Hospice building and by 1996 we had a lovely, large seminar room, which was to prove very useful for big meetings as it could seat up to fifty people comfortably. It was also a much better venue for our board meetings.

Not long after this extension had been completed it was decided to proceed with the ten-bed Residential Unit extension, at a projected overall cost of £1.25 million. By 1998 the new extension had been completed and fitted out and a new matron, Mrs Ruth Hardie, had been appointed in overall charge, with our current sister-in-charge being assigned to working in the local community, sourcing and interviewing prospective patients. At last we were a fully fledged residential hospice, and I really felt that we could start to make an outstanding difference to the care of incurably ill patients in the Dudley borough and surrounding areas.

We were lucky about this time to have another Stourbridge Rotarian, Clive Leyland, join us on the board. He had many years' experience as a paediatrician at Russell's Hall Hospital and would be able to provide the medical supervision and guidance needed.

Although I heard many glowing reports from people of the high standard of care and how much it had been appreciated, it was two or three years later, when my wife lost a best friend whose last week or two were spent in the Hospice, that we had an opportunity to see for ourselves the loving care that was being dispensed.

The official opening of the Residential Unit was not easy to arrange and was eventually scheduled to be performed by HRH the Duke of Gloucester at 2.15 p.m. on Thursday 29 November 2001. Two marquees were erected: a large one for the many volunteers who had helped us so loyally over the years in the shops, lottery and Hospice, and a smaller one, located next to the Hospice entrance for invited dignitaries. We had several of our own gazebos erected along the drive for members of the public, as well as one opposite the Hospice entrance for the school band that I had promised to organise.

The big day finally arrived. As we had expected, the Duke of Gloucester did not pull in the massive crowds that Princess Diana had done, but he did appear to be very genuinely interested in all that our chairman and matron had to tell him. With the band playing and the weather kind, everything went off well.

Towards the end of 2001, the board was called to attend a specially commissioned Risk Management Study, which cost quite a lot of money to set up and lasted over three hours. It consisted of a gentleman and his secretary talking through all sorts of possible risks on which we all had to concentrate. He eventually came to the Trading and Lottery Companies that I ran, and put forward the proposition that because they were not under the control of the main board, there may be a perceived risk.

I personally would have thought that the record of both Trading and Lottery Companies would have spoken for themselves, both having amassed vast amounts of money on a regular basis with no perceived problems that I was aware of. Unfortunately, I don't think others, who had worked many years where systems and procedures abound, saw it in quite the same light, unlike a hands-on businessman's approach of wanting everything kept as simple and straightforward as possible.

Over the following months I seemed to be bombarded with new requirements with regard to up-to-date monthly profit and loss accounts, prior notice of all board meetings, minutes of all meetings, annual accounts, accountant's reports, etc. Financial restrictions were also being placed on how much I could spend in any given year and on opening a new shop. I was also being advised to employ a chief executive, because board members could 'lose their houses' if anything went wrong: a scenario that I thought quite incredulous considering the performance of both companies and all the insurance facilities we had in place provided by a specialist medical insurance company. Furthermore, I am afraid that as everything was running so smoothly, I wouldn't have a clue when it came to telling this new executive of ours what to do. These recommendations would all cost money and would conflict with the extremely frugal way I had always developed and run the companies in order to generate every possible pound profit for the Hospice.

In my opinion, to run any business as financially successful two ingredients are always paramount: keep your costs to a minimum and your income to a maximum.

With the Hospice shops, I had always personally monitored every item of expenditure, and on the income front I had a monthly return itemising the daily, weekly and monthly takings, together with the monthly total for each shop for the

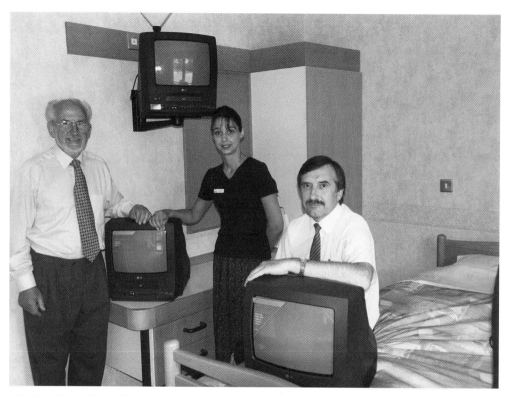

Geoff with Jackie Kelly, Matron of Mary Stevens Hospice, and his brother Bob Hill, managing director of Geoff Hill Limited, presenting ten colour television sets for the new Residential Unit, 1998.

previous year. This sheet of paper gave me a total overview of how each shop was performing, so that I could immediately address any individual shortfall in takings. At the same time it also gave me an ongoing indication of how the company would perform at the year end. In addition, I had also always personally monitored both shops and lottery bank accounts, transferring money from the current accounts into high-interest accounts on a regular basis. This, too, always gave me a very good indication of how much money we had made at any point during the year.

I had always given a full written report on each company at every board meeting. I had also given a full financial report, showing the exact cash position of how and where it was invested. Also, I elaborated on this with a verbal report on both companies, and if time permitted I would ask if there were any questions. Over the ten years that I was a board member I can honestly say that I can hardly remember any questions ever being asked. The chairman would always thank me and usually asked me to pass on the thanks of the board to the shops and lottery teams. This I always endeavoured to do. The Trading Company had run for ten years and the Lottery Company six years, both without any problems, and each had raised £1 million that year, the Hospice receiving £445,000 for the twelve months ending 31 March 2002. That was £95,000 more than the previous year. The profit from both companies had increased every year for ten years and as a businessman I could see no problem, so I just said, 'If it ain't broke why fix it?'

The success of my fundraising mission was brought home to me when coincidentally my charitable trust had applications for help from St Richard's Hospice, Worcester, and St Mary's Hospice, Birmingham. St Richard's had eight shops in a pleasant area that covered Worcester, Malvern, Broadway, Evesham, Pershore and Droitwich; and the total raised in the year from the shops and lottery was £120,000. St Mary's covered greater Birmingham, and its total raised was £136,210. In the same period our six Black Country shops and the lottery raised more than three times these amounts and should continue to do this sum, or more, every year for the foreseeable future.

I believe one thing which worried the board members was the fact that a couple of years previously, I had been diagnosed as having a leaking mitral valve in my heart, necessitating special medication. Once I had the correct medication the only inconvenience was that I needed to rest sometime in the afternoon, so I became a morning and evening person for work and meetings. I feel the board members were worried in case something happened to me suddenly, but I explained that I did not do anything like the amount of work that I had done in the earlier years when I was sourcing all the goods we sold in the shops.

I remember going to see a specialist in Birmingham who asked me how old I was and what I did. I said I was nearly 75, but probably was not your average 75-year-old. I mentioned some of the work I did in the electrical business that I was chairman of, and went on to tell him about the Hospice, my charitable trust, the Robert Parsons Trust and another two charities of which I was a trustee. The consultant took a deep breath, looked at me and said, 'Mr Hill, I'm twenty years younger than you and I'm exhausted just listening to you! Don't you think you ought to slow down a bit?' He did, however, add that I should avoid stress on all accounts.

I must admit that because I was not being left entirely alone to run and expand the businesses as I had done for the previous ten years or more, I was finding it quite stressful. With these thoughts in mind I told the Finance and General Purposes Committee that I would be leaving the Hospice. I did add, however, that I would always be available for help or advice should it ever be required.

In spite of having had differences of opinion with the board members over the last few months, I had always enjoyed their company over all the years, and fully respected their application and dedication, which had seen both the Day Hospice and, eventually, the wonderful Residential Unit evolve. Bryan Marshall, our very capable chairman, had been involved since the early stages, supervising its progress over all those years. Incidentally, at the same time that I was to leave the Hospice, he too was relinquishing the post of chairman. As someone said to me at the time, 'It's the end of an era!'

I have since been told that the money handed over to the Hospice from both shops and lottery has actually fallen by some £38,000 in the two years since I have left. In contrast, during my last six years there, I handed over an average increase of a massive £60,000 every year. With all due respect, as one of the volunteers once said, 'Perhaps this wily old hands-on businessman hadn't been doing too bad a job after all!'

And now a few final words about the Hospice, which may be important as years go by. I had always noticed that practically all of the hospices we visited had a 'home care' nursing team. I did at one stage bring this up at a Hospice board meeting, saying that I thought we should consider establishing such a team. However, the matron at the time did not exactly warm to the idea, so it went no further at that stage. I have helped Marie Curie Cancer Care over the years, and they run an extensive home-care team. Figures supplied to me during 2002 showed that they could provide 50 hours of 'specialised home care' for just £379. This meant that we could support eight or nine times as many patients at home for the cost of each patient in the Hospice Residential Unit. As Marie Curie also explained, if at all possible, three out of four terminally ill patients, understandably, prefer to spend their last weeks at home with their loved ones.

I recently saw a television programme where a man with a long-term terminal illness was attended to at home by a hospice home-care nurse; at the same time he would occasionally attend a hospice for specialised care. He could also phone at any time of day or night for help or advice if needed. To me, this sounded an ideal way to extend a hospice's facilities without incurring a too dramatic demand on resources. I sincerely hope this information may be taken heed of in future years, as and when funds permit.

Thanks to the awareness of the ongoing need for substantial Hospice funding, created first by the fundraising groups, and followed up by the shops, Christmas cards, lottery and professional hospice fundraisers, the general public, too, have responded magnificently with their own fundraising and memorial gifts, as well as with legacies, which in some cases have been quite substantial. This, I understand, has resulted in an appreciable amount of money building up in the Hospice 'Reserves Account'. It all guarantees the ongoing running and any future development of the Hospice for years to come in providing its specialised care for the terminally ill.

To finish on a positive note, I was recently approached in Kingswinford by a man who wanted to thank me for all the fundraising that I had organised for the Hospice. His mother had just died, spending her last six weeks there, and he was amazed by the wonderful care that had been administered to her during that time. As I am sure all the hundreds of other hospice volunteers will understand, it's at times like this that my twelve years' fundraising slog feels so worthwhile.

18

Leaving the Hospice

During the time that I came to my decision to make a complete break from the Hospice, including resigning from the main Hospice board, I never really thought through exactly what it would be like. It was only when I started going round the staff and volunteers of the Hospice, the lottery and all the shops, that I began to realise not only what it would mean to me, but also the impact it would have on all those dedicated people alongside whom I had worked for up to twelve years.

The lottery staff were the first to whom I broke the news. Although I thought that I had explained the position fully, after the initial shock one of them still followed me outside and said, 'You don't really mean that you are leaving us do you, Geoff?'

I was to get a similar reaction from the shops' staff and volunteers. In fact, Rupert, a volunteer at the Stourbridge shop, tried to persuade me to change my mind every time I went into the shop until my retirement. He kept saying, 'This is the shop that you created, Geoff, it just won't be the same without you.' It was lovely to hear his kind words, but I had to reply, 'Nothing lasts for ever and eventually it's time to move on.'

I had a lot of respect for the lottery staff and thought it would be nice if Sue and I took them and the volunteers out for a meal before we left. As soon as I suggested it to them they insisted that it would be them that took us out, and they would not be persuaded otherwise. A week or two later they kept their promise, and we had a lovely evening together, chatting and reminiscing. At the end of the evening they presented Sue with the most beautiful bouquet of flowers that she had ever seen. Certainly, they put in the shade those she had received from me over all our years together!

When it came to having a farewell ceremony for the Hospice shops' staff and volunteers, I thought that, as there were so many involved, the best thing would be to invite them round to our house one evening and hope that the weather would be kind to us, so that we could all sit outside and chat instead of being crammed indoors. The only problem was that we had a rather full diary and were going on a three-week touring holiday to France and Spain shortly after my retirement.

The next time I saw Gail, the shops' manageress, I outlined what Sue and I would like to do, but said that it would have to occur after our holiday. 'Forget it, Geoff,' was Gail's instant reply, 'it's all arranged, we're taking you out.' True to her word, a week or two later we had another wonderful evening with about thirty-five of the staff and volunteers. This time not only did Sue get a lovely bouquet of flowers but they gave me a £50 garden voucher as well. It was all so kind of them and enjoyable, but made the final parting even more difficult to handle.

When the word got round to all the staff and volunteers at the Hospice that I was leaving, some, who only came in for a few hours a week, became concerned as to whether they would see me again to say a final goodbye. Therefore, I asked the administrator to put a notice up saying that anyone who wished to, would be most welcome to visit our home for a drink and snacks in a couple of weeks' time. About twenty-five turned up, some coming with plants and presents, and once more we had a very memorable evening, culminating in our original day centre matron, Sara Hiam, saying a few kind words about our working relationship over eleven years or so. I also had two dozen letters and cards of thanks for my achievements at the Hospice from people who were unable to come, or who were on holiday, when these parties were held.

Finally, Sue and I were invited to the Hospice's boardroom one evening shortly after my retirement, where members and their wives were present. The chairman, Bryan Marshall, presented Sue and me with a beautiful large, cut-glass bowl appropriately engraved with their thanks for our fundraising achievements over the years. I expressed our thanks and my pleasure in having worked with them all for so many years and added one final word of warning: to be very careful if they intended to appoint a person on a high salary to oversee the shops and lottery operations, particularly as they were unlikely to know very much about either of these well-staffed and exceedingly well-run organisations. I thought that the fourth farewell night had finally, well and truly, wrapped up my leaving of the Hospice, but there was still one more unexpected surprise in store for me.

It was many weeks later, during the run-up to Christmas, that Sue and I had to drop into the lottery office for some reason. Jenny and Debbie, the main operatives there, said that they would like to pop round home sometime to see us for a few minutes. Sue arranged a convenient afternoon and they came in for what I thought would be a cup of tea and a final chat. They were with us for a few minutes, and then suddenly presented me with a gift, which I opened and found to be a beautiful A4-size photo album. I thought it must be a Christmas present and went to thank them for it, when they told me to open it. I did so, and just couldn't believe what I saw. There were thirty pages of facts, figures and photographs of the lottery, from since the first draw in July 1996, when there were 3,160 players for the £2,000 worth of prizes, to the last sheet of statistics, which showed 10,923 players for the £3,000 worth of prizes, and a massive £2,835,794 taken in the 321 weekly draws since the lottery's inception! Details of the first member of the lottery, and the 20,302th and last member's registration form were also included. There were also many photos of my staff, and caricatures and cut-outs of all the office staff over the years, plus office volunteers, collectors and supervisors. It must have taken them weeks to put it all together.

Finally, there was a lovely poem composed by Sue Roden, the excellent field manager I'd had until she retired to South Wales some twelve months before my retirement. While she was at the Hospice, Sue Roden had compiled and published her own book of poems, largely about the Hospice and the lottery. This was the one she wrote about me:

> The story began some ten years ago,
> The birth of the Hospice that we all know,
> The building took place, a wonderful sight,
> The money to raise, would be quite a fight.
>
> Geoff Hill is the one, he's always been there,
> He's never been known to just stand and stare,
> A job to be done, he's there on the spot,
> All his appointments, right on the dot.
>
> Then Geoff had a vision, much money to make,
> Sponsor a lottery, for the Hospice's sake,
> A team of canvassers flooded the streets,
> Lots of targets for them to meet.
>
> Computers were bought and office was staffed,
> We'll get some collectors, nobody laughed.
> With your guiding hand the lottery has grown,
> Now six years on, how time has flown.
>
> Your boundless energy, we've all admired,
> Your fundraising prowess, how you inspired.
> And now it's time to rest a while,
> Enjoy your retirement, look back and smile.
>
> Reflect on the goodness that you have achieved,
> The money from you that the Hospice received,
> Thank you for all the time you have given
> For the plight of others, you've always been driven.

Sue Roden

The book finished with lovely compiled photographs of me with all the final staff plus Sue Roden, and a further two pages where lots of the staff and volunteers had inserted farewell messages. Quite a number of the messages suggested that, knowing me, it would more than likely not be a quiet retirement. They were probably right!

19

The Geoff Hill
Charitable Trust

During the last year or two of my working full time at the electrical store, I thought it would be useful to be more involved in charity work when I retired. Thinking of how I could help the dozens of needy causes which never get any help at all, I hit on the idea of forming the Geoff Hill Charitable Trust, using 10 per cent of my shares in Geoff Hill Limited. This would mean that every year approximately £15,000 would be available for distribution to all these groups. Little did I know that I would become so involved in fundraising for the Hospice that it would become virtually a full-time job, leaving me no time to get my own trust off the ground.

It was some seven years later, in the early part of 1997, that I had the charity officially set up and running, managing to get dividends allocated to it from my shop trading years 1995/6 and 1996/7. I had my wife, Sue, and brother, Robert, as fellow trustees, but as Robert was always very busy running the electrical store, Sue had to do all the back-up office work of letters and bookkeeping for the trust. I have nearly always endeavoured to research all the applications myself and make decisions on who receives what.

I soon found that if the trust had no publicity other than details in our showroom, or on invoices, advertisements, etc, the applications came in very slowly and practically everyone received a grant. The trouble with this was that I felt that the number of needy groups and organisations that didn't know about the Trust's existence could be far larger. On the other hand, when there was publicity that the Trust had funds available for allocation, the floodgates opened and during the next fourteen days or so I would have fifty to sixty letters in my tray! It then became difficult to decide which were the neediest applicants and how much to grant them.

At the end of 1997 I had a chat with Jeff Jephcott, editor of the News Group. He arranged for my trust to be promoted throughout 1998 and to give away £1,000 each month through the Stourbridge, Dudley and Halesowen free newspapers. It worked quite well and all through the year I was never short of needy recipients for the monthly grants. I realised quite early on that I would have to exclude individuals, as they would be too difficult to monitor. I also had to refuse organisations which were outside the catchment area of the electrical store. This was

*Geoff with the Mayor of Dudley,
Councillor Margaret Wilson, at a
Queen's Golden Jubilee draw of fifty
£100 prizes, 2002.*

difficult at times, as national publications carry details of charitable trusts and do not always specify the areas in which grants are applicable.

In March 2000 Linda Cartwright and Robert Billingham, two of the Geoff Hill Limited directors, were also appointed as trustees. In October of that year, to mark the fortieth anniversary of the superstore, I decided to repeat the celebration that I had for thirty years' trading, only this time giving away forty colour TVs and financing them from the charitable trust. Once again it was a great night, held in the Methodist hall across the road from my showroom, but now in a brand new building. About eighty charities and needy causes came and Tommy Mundon again willingly accepted my invitation to carry out the draw. This time we decided that we should have consolation prizes for those who were unsuccessful in the main draw, and the shop staff saw that a supply of Sony Walkmans was available so that no one went home empty-handed.

The next multiple handout of prizes came in 2002, when it was decided to commemorate the Queen's fifty years on the throne by giving away fifty £100 cheques to each of the lucky winners. A week or two before the exact date, we held our 'Golden Jubilee Grand Draw', and the Mayor of Dudley, Councillor Margaret Wilson, kindly came along to draw the winning tickets. The £100 prizes enabled many of the groups to celebrate the event in a much better fashion than they would otherwise have done and we had lots of 'thank you' letters to that effect.

By the end of 2005 the trust had disposed of £150,000 to over 550 different groups and charities. It's really amazing how many diverse organisations are out there in the local community. Some are just branches of national organisations, but the vast majority are small groups, most of which get no help at all from the local authority. Many have members who are too old or not in good enough health to do much fundraising for themselves.

I have supported a few charities for the blind and also one or two for the deaf. In particular, I have helped the Deaf/Blind Charity, which have their head office at Peterborough, on a regular basis, as I have always felt that this combination of disabilities must surely be one of the most difficult afflictions to live with. I have been invited over to the head office on more than one occasion to see exactly how they operate; one day I shall find time to accept their kind offer. Mary Stevens Hospice, Compton Hospice and our local hospitals at Russells Hall, Wordsley and the Corbett Hospital have all been substantially helped, as well as many cancer and other health-related charities.

There are also clubs for the elderly that are always looking for a meal out or a trip to the country or seaside. At the other end of the spectrum, many schools and youngsters' football clubs have received donations. I've always especially tried to help the underprivileged areas in the borough. Add to this the scouts' groups, guides, theatrical societies, churches and the many different types of sporting clubs, and I'm sure you'll begin to realise how the vast number of requests is generated.

Although I have always restricted the grants to local groups and charities, I do confess to having made one exception, every year paying the airfares for two of the Chernobyl children to come over here. Reading of their plight at home is quite horrific. Sue and I have been able to meet them each year, and had some of these lovely children round to our house for Christmas 2002. At Christmas 2003 we were invited one evening to a party at Lye Football Club for all the Chernobyl children, their carers and the organisers. They had only been here for a week but all looked radiant, with the girls in new party dresses and shoes, and all had had their hair styled; they all looked so happy. We were able to have a long chat to their Russian

Sue and Geoff being presented with certificates by two Chernobyl children, Aliksander Xasiukevich and Daria Unqur, at a party just before the end of their visit in 2005.

interpreter, who was a teacher back home. She even brought us a beautifully illustrated book of school children's stories, with English interpretation and a lovely, typically Russian, hand-painted salt cellar.

The ground where the children live is still toxic, so that all the food grown there is still contaminating their bodies. Unbelievably, it is said that the month that they spend here, eating clean, wholesome food, adds an extra two years to their life expectancy.

In August 2004 and 2005 Sue and I were invited to the leaving party at Kinver for twenty-seven children who had been here a month and were about to return home. They were all so wonderfully fit and happy and well behaved it was a joy to see. However, we were both saddened to think of the austere lifestyle that had been described to us in detail and to which they would be returning.

The most heart-warming happening that I have experienced with my donations was when Sue and I were in Boston, USA, on a Stourbridge Rotary Club exchange with Sturbridge Rotary Club. Out of the blue I received a phone call from a quite young family man who had been diagnosed with an incurable form of cancer. Via the Internet, his wife had found that there was a consultant in Mexico who had cured this particular type of cancer, and so I had helped towards his fundraising for the trip. His phone call to me some months later was to say that, after having the treatment, he had returned to the specialist back home and had now been pronounced clear of the cancer. It was such a wonderful moment and he was so happy and appreciative. That brief phone call really made our trip!

It's lovely when I have been able to help a group, often in only some fairly small way, towards their new ambulance, minibus or building extension, etc., and they invite Sue and me along months or even years later when it is all finally in use.

By 2005 the increased competition from Internet sites and supermarkets selling electrical items had an effect on the profit generated at the Geoff Hill store. The dividend had to be halved to £7,500. Fortunately, by then, however, the money that I had put in personally over the years had built up enough for me to purchase commercial property, the annual income from which is £18,000. This means that now some £2,000 per month is available for allocation to charities. Over the years I have received a few donations quite unexpectedly from people who appreciate what I am trying to do in the community and want to help. Dudley and District Business Club, of which I am a member, have made donations to the Geoff Hill Charitable Trust on each of their annual charity evenings. Most of the members are small-business people, like ourselves, and are grateful for what we, as a local firm, are trying to achieve.

I might add that there must be many people in the locality who have personal funds that they can't possibly spend in their lifetime. As you can't take it with you when you go, it seems an eminently sensible thing to give some of it away during your life, getting the pleasure of helping people who, in most cases, desperately need it.

I recently read an article about an American businessman who had given away several million dollars over the last few years. The article concluded with him saying, 'I thought that I had enjoyed making all this money, but giving it away has been far more enjoyable!' I think that I agree with him; it's like being Father Christmas all the year round. If you are a retired, wealthy businessman, think about it.

20

The Robert Parsons Story

It was at the end of July 2000 that one of my staff, Robert Parsons, an 18-year-old driver's mate at the Geoff Hill Electrical Store, was struck down by an unbelievably swift and devastating illness. He went to bed early with head pains and was sick during the night. The next morning his father, John, saw spots on his body which were noticeably getting worse and immediately suspected meningitis. He dialled 999 and Robert was rushed by ambulance to Russells Hall Hospital, where he was diagnosed as having a severe form of meningitis known as meningococcal septicaemia. He was immediately taken into intensive care and at one stage his parents were told that there was only a 10 per cent chance of his surviving.

After a few days Sue and I visited Robert and met his mother, father and sister in an adjacent waiting room. In a little while we were allowed to go in to see Robert, who was asleep and heavily sedated. His father lifted the sheet covering his legs to show us that they were totally black below the knees, as were his hands, forearms and the end of his nose too. To save his life, both legs, hands and forearms had to be amputated. There were even more complications because he had also contracted the hospital superbug, MRSA, which alone claims several thousands of lives every year.

After a month or more in intensive care he was eventually transferred to Selly Oak Hospital, on the outskirts of Birmingham, to have more treatment and plastic surgery on his severed limbs. However, there was more bad news to come, as it was discovered that his knee joints were incapable of supporting his bodyweight; so Robert had to undergo further amputations, removing the lower legs completely.

Throughout this thoroughly traumatic time I never heard him complain once. In fact, the first time that Sue and I went to visit him at Selly Oak, before I could ask Robert how he was, he was already enquiring about my health. My staff, particularly those who had worked with him in the stores and on deliveries, were very good, and after working until 6 p.m. at the showroom they would often go all the way over to Selly Oak to visit him.

By early October 2000 it was obvious that, with his determination and the support of his family, he was certainly going to make a life for himself. It occurred to me then that he would need a lot of money to do it. I was having recurring trouble with my lower back at the time, and on a visit to a physiotherapist I knew at Kingswinford, I told him Robert's story and asked if he knew how much a full set of 'bionic' arms and legs would cost. He thought about it for a little while and said that it could well be in the region of £50,000. This would be a tremendous amount

Geoff speaks to a packed audience at Amblecote Methodist Church Hall to launch the Robert Parsons Appeal before donating television sets to local worthy causes, 2000.

of money to Robert's family, and in addition there could well be many other specialised items of equipment that he would require over the years.

I decided there and then that the only way to protect his future would be to launch an appeal. The one thing that made me hesitant was that Robert's family had always appeared to me as very private people. I wondered if they would be prepared to handle the press, who could be quite intrusive with phone calls or even calling at the house, when the family had already so much to cope with. I wasn't at all sure that they would welcome this aspect of a full-blown fundraising campaign.

There was only one way for me to find out, and that was to speak to Robert's father, John. I explained in detail what I would like to do, also adding that I would like to launch the appeal the following Tuesday evening at the Methodist hall, where I would be giving away forty TVs to celebrate forty years' trading. About 150 people would be present, representing some 80 different charities. I also had Tommy Mundon coming to help with the draw. I asked John to talk it over with Robert and the family, and to let me know if it would be in order to proceed, as far as they were concerned.

The following morning John rang back to say that they were all delighted and excited at my suggestion. I was very pleased to hear this and asked if he would like to come along to the launch and give a short talk about Robert from a father's point of view. He readily agreed to do this, but added that he would have to leave immediately afterwards to visit Robert at Selly Oak.

Tuesday night came and people started to fill the hall, where there was now a large pyramid of forty televisions built up on the stage. My staff were serving coffee and biscuits and by 7.30 p.m. we were all ready to start. Tommy Mundon hadn't arrived, but in this case it didn't matter because I wanted to start with the appeal for Robert. I stood behind the raffle drum and explained to everyone that I had something serious to talk about before proceeding with the draw. I then told the story of Robert and what he had gone through, and said that his father was here to fill in other details; but more importantly, I wanted to kick-start a fund for him that night. I then handed John a cheque to start off the fund.

I hadn't mentioned a figure to anyone, not even my wife Sue, but felt so strongly for Robert and admired his positive, uncomplaining attitude so much, that I had written out a cheque for £10,000. John was absolutely amazed when he saw the cheque. After thanking me, he went on to give a brief account of what Robert had gone through during those last few horrendous weeks. As soon as John had finished and left with his wife to visit Robert, my staff passed a couple of buckets around the audience, who were still quite stunned by what they had just heard. In the next 10 minutes or so an extra £600 had been collected, including £20 from each member of my staff who was present. By then, Tommy Munden had arrived and the evening moved towards the fun part and the disposal of the television sets, although one or two of the recipients kindly felt that they had to say something about Robert over the microphone as they came forward to collect their prizes.

Geoff with Robert Parsons at Rowley Regis Centre, where £2,000 was raised for his appeal fund, 2001.

Within days the story was emblazoned over the front pages of the *Express & Star* and *Stourbridge News*, money started rolling into the showroom. I had decided by then to set up a Robert Parsons Account within the Geoff Hill Charitable Trust, so that all money donated to Robert would accumulate in a tax-free environment. One of the great benefits of this was that we could apply for Gift Aid on all donations from tax-payers, and this meant that eventually an extra 28p for every £1 would go into Robert's fund directly from the government! From Robert's point of view, the possible downside was that the money would not be in his own bank account for him to spend as he chose. After careful consideration of his long-term welfare, and in line with the wishes of his many thousands of benefactors, it would be decided by the trustees to allocate it to Robert as they saw fit.

During the following weeks money came in from all quarters. It was during the run-up to Christmas and the busiest time of the year at the Geoff Hill store. Every day at least one member of staff had to spend all their time receiving and counting cash and cheques from generous people who descended on the showroom in droves. Sometimes it would be a plastic bucket of coins collected around pubs, other times a cheque for up to £100, occasionally just a small amount from a pensioner with tears in their eyes. It was obviously very emotional for a lot of the people and my staff had to respect this, trying to give each person a little bit of time to talk about how Robert was doing and how much money the fund had raised.

From my side, many firms and clubs had gone to a lot of trouble raising up to £1,000 or more, wanting me if at all possible to go along personally to collect the money and tell them about Robert. I always did this, but it became quite a balancing act with the daily schedule of running the Hospice shops, the lottery and selling all the Christmas cards, etc., to name but a few of my tasks. One day, I remember, I was at a Wolverhampton Business Club breakfast meeting at 7 a.m., followed by a Stourbridge Rotary Club presentation at lunchtime and, later, at about 10 p.m., at a further collection made during the interval of an entertainment show at a club in Old Hill!

The money came in at such a rate the £50,000 target was reached in just fifty days. It was all quite unbelievable at the time. Every few days I was able to update the local press on all the latest fundraising events that had been staged for Robert. At the end of every press release I would have another appeal asking for more funds and stating where to bring or post them to.

I targeted Beacon Radio in Wolverhampton and one or two Birmingham radio stations; all were very helpful in giving me interviews on air about Robert. With their help, money came in from all over the Midlands area, the farthest away being Stratford-upon-Avon.

The Geoff Hill staff wanted to do their bit and organised a night of entertainment at the Stewpony Hotel, and several local groups and solo entertainers volunteered to perform free of charge. It was soon a 'sell out', and with a giant raffle of items donated by the public to help raise money for Robert, we were able to do just that and have a great night's entertainment as well.

I was often out several nights each week, collecting money at special events, but one night stood out above others for the sheer generosity of the people. It was at an

Geoff at Lower Gornal British Legion Hall with Cedric and Muriel Grove, who raised £4,169 for the Robert Parsons Appeal, 2001.

event organised by Cedric Grove and his wife, Muriel, at Lower Gornal British Legion. They had been arranging events there for more than twenty-five years, raising money for many different charities in the process. Cedric told Sue and me what time to arrive, saying that a raffle would be held during the interval and that afterwards he would present the proceeds to me on stage. I thanked him very much and asked if he would like me to say a few words about Robert after the presentation. Cedric said, 'That will be fine.'

On the night I briefly recounted the story to date about Robert, adding how brave he had been throughout this whole tragic experience. It was when I came down from the stage to join Sue in the audience that, suddenly, people started giving us extra donations of £5, £10 and £20 notes – one person even gave a £50 note. In about 7 or 8 minutes we had a total of £220 to add to the £310 raised in the raffle, making it £530 on the night. I don't think Sue and I will ever forget those few minutes of generosity on the part of very caring and warm-hearted people.

This was not to be the last we were to hear from Cedric Grove. Later, he said that he would like to put on a special fundraising night for Robert, adding that he was hoping to get the Three Degrees to entertain. In case you don't know, the Three Degrees were one of the best and most sought-after female singing groups of the last twenty or more years; and they were going to perform at Lower Gornal British Legion! At first it just didn't make sense; I thought that there was possibly a Three Degrees look-alike group who tried to sing like their world-famous namesakes. But no, it really was the Three Degrees that Cedric was talking about – he seemed to know the agent who handled bookings for them in this country. If they could get a booking here (normally costing about £10,000), they would do this gig only for expenses. As well as this, Cedric wanted to do a big raffle for Robert, having the tickets printed so that he could sell them for several weeks in advance of the event.

Tragically, we had the terrible happenings in New York on 11 September, just a week or so before the show. This put an automatic stop on most people flying out from the USA and the Three Degrees were, unfortunately, included among them. Undaunted, Cedric found that the equally famous male group, the Drifters, were in Blackpool and were willing to come down and perform for Robert on the night. This they did, and they were absolutely brilliant, performing for over an hour and taking several encores. I was finally presented with a cheque for well over £4,000, raised as a result of Cedric's, his wife's and their friends' efforts, and also all the other people there on the night.

I would like to recount the story of one other of the many fundraising events that were put on for Robert, and that was at the complete opposite end of the scale in terms of money raised. It was as a result of a phone conversation I had with a Mr Jack Smith, who lived with his wife, Mary, in sheltered accommodation in Pedmore, Stourbridge. Mary had decided to raffle off all the presents she had received for her 90th birthday. As neither she nor Jack, who was 89, was able to leave their home, the £70 they raised was a real labour of love. They were a delightful couple and I remember Jack insisting on putting on a tie and neatly buttoning up his cardigan before Sue took a photo of them both, which was published in the *Stourbridge News* the following week, with an appropriate write-up. Sadly, Mary died not long afterwards, but they so appreciated and enjoyed our visit, as well as the unexpected publicity that was generated.

When Robert was finally discharged from hospital and settled in at home, I tried to pop round in the evenings for an hour or so, to see how he was doing and to keep him up to date with the total of money in the trust. He and his father, John, had attended one or two of the fundraising events that were still being held for him. The whole family appeared very appreciative of the work I had put into the fundraising, also of the wonderful response from the Black Country people. £100,000 was raised in only 100 days and, although it was starting to slow down, money was still coming in at quite a steady rate.

Early in 2001 we started to claim the 28p in the £1 Gift Aid on all donations. I managed to get the local newspapers to run a coupon in their editorials for people to fill in if they had made a donation, so that we could claim the extra cash. Meanwhile, the staff at the shop telephoned or wrote to all they knew who had made donations, despatching forms where appropriate. All our efforts paid off and we eventually received over £20,000 back in Gift Aid.

The fact that Robert's money was in the charitable trust was to help in other ways too. There was a young man, Sat Bala, who had raised tremendous amounts of money for Robert by performing in the street in Wolverhampton town centre. I used to ring him up and thank him for the wonderful amounts (often over £1,000) that he had raised. One day he said how disappointed he was that the building society with which he dealt and which he knew had a charity account, had refused to make a grant to Robert on the grounds that they didn't make donations to individuals. I said that actually the money was not being paid direct to Robert, but to the Geoff Hill Charitable Trust, so I thought that I might be able to get them to view it in a different light. I phoned the building society and spoke to a very nice young lady, explaining the situation to her. She passed on my comments to the people who administered the charity division; lo and behold, a few days later a cheque for £500 arrived. Both Sat Bala and I were delighted.

Another occasion when having the money secured in the charitable trust proved useful, was when I visited Robert one evening and his father explained to me about the ground-floor extension to the house that was desperately needed. He added that Dudley Council had heard about the vast amount of money that had been donated for Robert's welfare and expected the extension to be paid for from this source. I immediately said to John that it was possible that the trust wouldn't sanction the payment and that I would ring him back the next day. After speaking to the appropriate solicitor and tax specialist who had set up the trust, they both agreed with me, in that an extension would be adding value to the house owned by Robert's father and would not be of value to Robert when he was able to live elsewhere. Later, I had a letter from Dudley Council suggesting payment by the trust, but heard nothing further from them after replying and explaining the position as we saw it. This bit of quick thinking saved Robert some £15,000 to £20,000.

After the fund had been running for some four months and the total had soared to £129,000, a charity football match was staged at Stourbridge Football Club between Stourbridge Old Stars and Aston Villa Old Stars. I was also able, on this occasion, to help publicise Mary Stevens Hospice and raise money for it, by having various stalls at the ground. I was able to put a piece in the programme about Robert, as well as one about the Hospice, explaining how people could help either of these worthy causes. Robert's parents were also

Geoff dressed in Aston Villa shirt, with Alan Pitt, to promote the Stourbridge All Stars vs Aston Villa All Stars football match, 2001.

able to insert a piece about him from a family perspective. The match itself was well attended and proved very close and exciting. Robert was introduced to both the teams when it was over. At the end of the day everyone had had a great time, and on this occasion both of my charitable causes had raised quite a few more pounds.

Another highlight of the fundraising was when, after a few phone calls, the BBC Midland News crew agreed to come and film Robert in his home. Afterwards they came over to the Geoff Hill showroom, where I was able to say a few words about his fund. It was when they were filming Robert's dad and he said that he and his wife had thought they might have to sell their home to raise the cash needed for Robert's limbs, that I realised how important it must have been for the whole family when the fund was started.

While Robert was in hospital, there was a young lad he had befriended who, sadly, did not survive. I think this was something that Robert, being the resilient lad that he is, latched on to, realising that he was the lucky one who was still alive. With his mentality unimpaired, he seemed determined to lead as full and normal a life as was humanly possible.

He continued to make steady progress, with regular physiotherapy sessions at the local hospital. In his spare time, with adaptations taped onto his arms by his father, he tapped out well over 200 'thank you' letters on the computer. I often thought what a blessing it was for him that we were in the computer age, because he could fill endless hours on his machine.

The next highlight in Robert's return to a normal life came almost twelve months to the day after his being struck down with the appalling illness. It was the day that he took delivery of his specially converted green Ford Mondeo car. I had approached the Pedmore Sporting Club at Stourbridge, which help lots of needy causes in the area, to ask if they would make a donation to Robert's fund. They usually preferred to pay for something rather than just to hand over money, and so I had suggested that they might like to fund the conversion costs for Robert's new car. They readily agreed to this and very kindly paid the £3,500 fee when the car was converted.

It was a few days into August 2001, I was at Robert's house with the press, two gentlemen from the Pedmore Sporting Club, Robert and his wonderful new car. After appropriate photos had been taken, Robert said, 'Would you like me to take you for a spin in it, Geoff?' I replied, 'Oh, yes please, Robert, that would be great.' Quick as a flash, we were out of his quite narrow and sloping drive for a tour through the Norton estate and up the Kidderminster road. It quite amazed me how adept and confident this 19-year-old was, having only taken delivery of the vehicle some three days before.

When we returned to his house, he reversed down the drive and at the first attempt parked the car quite close to the wall, so that he had sufficient room to get out with his artificial legs, which were rather long for this purpose. As you can imagine, I was very surprised and pleased by his performance, and delighted that at last he had something that would give him countless hours of pleasure for many years to come.

It was sad, in a way, that for the next two years neither the shop staff nor Sue and I saw virtually anything of Robert. When the press enquired for information I would try to explain what a private family they were and that he just wanted to return to a

Geoff with Robert Parsons, on taking delivery of his specially converted Ford Mondeo car, August 2001. (Express & Star)

normal, publicity-free life. This was fine up to a point, but every week, sometimes every day, people were asking me how Robert was doing. I was finding it increasingly difficult to give satisfactory answers when I hadn't seen him for so long.

It was then that I decided to write to Robert, asking if he would like to attend the next charitable trust meeting so that we could get a better understanding of his financial needs. Robert and his father attended the meeting, in September 2003. It was an ideal time to say to Robert that although we all respected his desire for anonymity, people who had supported him so generously were genuinely concerned about his ongoing welfare. Robert agreed to provide a summary about twice a year, so that the press could update all supporters on his current progress and interests. I told him that we could also add that the fund was still open for donations and provide details of where to send them.

True to his word, a short time afterwards Robert sent me an account of his life to date; the one thing that stood out to me, when I read it, was that he had driven 20,000 miles in the car in the two years that he had had it. He has now driven over 50,000 miles. Given his condition, I found this truly amazing. He's quite a lad!

21

The Dudley Hope Trust

It was in October 1997 that Jeff Jephcott, editor of the *Stourbridge News*, phoned me to see if I could help with an appeal that had been launched by the Dudley Council for Voluntary Services (or DCVS as they are known), in Brierley Hill. It was the start of the run-up to Christmas and it appeared that there were some 500 children in the Dudley borough who were unlikely to get any presents that Christmas. Jeff wondered if I could help by contributing to a fund initiated to raise £5,000, to buy 500 presents at an average of £10 each. I had not long established my charitable trust and was quite happy to donate £500 to what I saw at the time as being a very worthwhile cause, when most children seemed to have far too many gifts, as compared to my own fairly austere childhood. The fundraising was very successful, thanks to plenty of publicity from the News Group newspapers, and 500 presents were purchased, and presented at Christmas to grateful recipients.

On 9 April 1998 it was decided to have a meeting at the DCVS offices in Brierley Hill, to discuss the viability of forming a charitable community trust for the Dudley borough. Those present officially decided that a trust would be formed to be known as the Hope Community Trust, its object being to raise as much money as possible throughout the year, with £5,000 being earmarked to purchase the 500 Christmas presents, while the rest of the disposable funds could be used during the year to help young people in general, up to the age of 18. I approached my accountants, Nicklins of Halesowen, to see if they would help, and hopefully act as accountants for the trust. This they kindly did.

For the first year or two we had some help from the Dudley Chamber of Commerce, but this seemed to disappear once they became incorporated into the much larger Black Country Chamber. During 1998 Hamiltons the accountants staged a 'Ladies' Day' fundraising event which raised a massive £7,391 for us. I was too busy with all my Hospice commitments to carry out any fundraising for the trust, but from 1998 onwards, every year I made a donation of £1,000 about October to kick-start the trust's Santa Appeal section.

It was in July 1998 that I managed to get Harvey Owen, a partner at Nicklins, to join the trust board, and he was to prove an invaluable asset. Not only was he able to take over the problems of treasurer, but he proved to be a great fundraiser for the trust by putting on an annual Hope Ball for his business clients, which always raised many thousands of pounds.

The trust performed quite well for a few years, and each Christmas, as well as handing out 500 or so presents, we were able to arrange for lots of children to visit pantomimes and for others to have discos. During the remainder of the year our very capable secretary, Gill Cooper of DCVS, would acquaint us with other applicants who had requested help and we would endeavour to stretch our limited resources to assist as many needy causes as possible.

Unfortunately, 2002 was a very bad year on the fundraising front, when one or two events had to be cancelled and our income fell quite appreciably, so the number of children for whom we brought presents was limited to about 250. By now we were having to spend closer to £20 to buy appropriate presents, and the DCVS staff were presenting the lucky children with a list so that they could actually choose the present that they would like for Christmas.

However, 2003 started more promisingly, and the Mayor of Dudley, Councillor Rosemary Tomkinson, kindly agreed to support our trust during her year of office, which helped us not only financially but also on the publicity front.

By 2004, I thought it might be nice to raise some money for the Hope Trust by opening our garden to the public when the rhododendrons and azaleas were at their best, choosing Sunday 23 May, from 1 p.m. to 5 p.m. We kept our fingers crossed that the weather would be fine on the day. As with the openings in previous years for Stourbridge Rotary Club, we obtained large quantities of plants and hanging baskets for a plant sale, and Sue spent the greater part of three days baking a variety

Open garden party at Geoff's home, Tinkers Cottage, Lawnswood, Wordsley, in aid of the Dudley Hope Charity.

Geoff presents a High Hopes rose to the Mayor of Dudley, Councillor Rosemary Tomkinson, at the 2004 garden party.

of cakes and scones. As it got nearer the day the weather forecast was good and we became concerned that there would not be room for everyone to park, so Sue obtained permission to use a field just across the road from our house. It was a good job that we did, because the field was filled with cars in the first hour.

The Mayor and Mayoress kindly came along, to add a bit of glamour to the afternoon, and we were able to present the lady Mayor with a climbing rose called High Hopes which, as well as being appropriate for our charity, also highly delighted the Mayor, who was a very keen gardener. We staged a big raffle and, with the entrance fee, plant stall, tea and cakes, plus another £750 in matched funding from the Barclays Bank girls who kindly helped us on the day, we raised a massive £2,860 and had some 600 visitors to our garden.

In May 2005 I managed to persuade Sue to embark on another Open Garden event. This time, to make it easy for us, I suggested to Stourbridge Rotary Club president, David Collins, that it might be a good idea if it were billed as a Rotary event. He immediately warmed to the idea, so we had the help of several Rotarians in their yellow tabards, parking the cars in the field for us, while the Rotary wives helped Sue by bringing lots of homemade cakes and generally helping out wherever needed on the day. This time our local nurseries were particularly generous with their donation of plants and hanging baskets, and with the help of many other kind people donating plants we made a total of £500 on the plant stall alone.

So many cakes had been made that we put on an extra, impromptu cake stall, which, together with all the tea and cakes sold, the raffle, entrance fees and the Barclays Bank funding, brought in a massive total of £3,100. It could have been more, because after a quite threatening day weather-wise, the heavens eventually opened at about 3.45 p.m., bringing the proceedings to an abrupt end. Our newly appointed Mayor and Mayoress of Dudley, Councillor Ian Kettle and his wife, Joan, joined us and enjoyed participating in all the activities.

As well as the money that was raised, we were able to publicise the charity with new, 6ft-tall portable display posters for the Hope Trust. A photograph and write-up on the front of the *Express & Star* the next night helped us as well.

22

Stourbridge Rotary Club

I had heard about Rotary Clubs during my years in business, but had never felt that I had enough spare time to join one. My old school friend, Jim Higgs, had joined Stourbridge Rotary Club in 1991, so at the beginning of 1993 I accepted the invitation to go along for an interview. To be quite honest, I was very much into putting on fundraising events at the time and my motive in joining was as much for the help they might give me, as for what I could do to assist Rotary.

Stourbridge Rotary Club is a rather large club, with some seventy or more members who meet every Wednesday lunchtime at the Talbot Hotel, Stourbridge. We have a lunch together, followed by a few announcements, with a speaker for the last 30 minutes or so in order that the meeting finishes at around 2 p.m.

I soon became familiar with the seventy or so other Stourbridge Rotarians and found them to be a very friendly group, as did Sue when she started attending Rotary Wives meetings and the many joint social evenings that we were to have together. Over the years I have always been on their social service committee, which make grants to local people and organisations and also put on occasional fundraising events to swell the coffers of the club so that it may carry on with its good work.

Sue and I have tried to help in fundraising or social events by staging one from time to time at home. Sometimes it's been Pâté and Punch at Christmas time, when our heavily timbered house looks at its best, with log fires burning brightly in large, old, stone fireplaces; other times, usually towards the end of May, when the garden is suddenly a blaze of colour from dozens of massive azaleas and rhododendrons, which were planted some

Geoff with his wife Sue, the night he received the Rotary Paul Harris Fellow Award, 14 March 2001.

seventy years ago and present a magical display. If you're lucky, the bluebell walk through the surrounding woodland is still a carpet of blue, and if it's a nice day there's a hammock in which to relax and take it all in.

We staged a couple of fundraising events just for the Rotary Club at this particular time of the year: one in 2000 and the other in 2003. Sue served tea and homemade cakes, while I organised a large bring and buy plant stall. I organised a raffle as well, and for the first event we raised £700 in just two hours.

In 2003 we went one better. Realising that Barclays Bank had a community fund, and having been a good customer of theirs for forty-three years, I approached the staff at the Stourbridge branch and found that they would be pleased to help on the day, and that the bank would offer matched funding up to £750. The weather was kind and we had a great couple of hours and made £746 for Breakthrough Breast Cancer, the Rotary Wives' charity, which Barclays matched to make £1,492.

Every year we have a lunchtime charity auction to which all the Rotarians bring an item for auction. Men are not very imaginative in this department and usually grab a bottle of wine or whisky to get them out of trouble. Several years ago, I remember, the president appealed for us to stretch ourselves to provide something different, so I decided to auction a week at our holiday home in mid-Wales. I passed around a sheet with appropriate photos of the pretty spot, and each year it has raised about £250. It has been very satisfying to introduce our Rotary friends to the beauty of this area.

We have had so many lovely Rotary evenings over the past ten years, but one night stood out for me from all the others. It was the president's Ladies' Evening, staged in the beautiful, old, panelled and chandeliered hall of Oldswinford School on 14 March 2001. We had just finished dinner when my old school friend, Jim Higgs, stood up and began talking at length about a young man that he used to know who had three interests in life: cycle racing, amateur dramatics and girls – not always in that order!

This young man also had lots of jobs; and as he had lots of girlfriends he didn't know whether a new job required a new girlfriend or a new girlfriend necessitated a change of job! Jim continued for another 10 or 15 minutes, and I was wondering where on earth it was all leading to, as there was no mention of this in the evening programme.

Eventually, after he had touched on my Hospice work and the Robert Parsons fund in a very veiled fashion, Jim was interrupted by our president, Michael Billingham, and the mystery was revealed. He announced that I had been unanimously chosen by the Stourbridge Rotary Council to be awarded the top Rotary International Award by being made a Paul Harris Fellow, named after the founder of Rotary International some 100 years ago. The special medal was hung round my neck and an appropriate Rotary lapel badge was inserted in my jacket, and everyone started applauding. It was all a total surprise to me. Then, while still almost speechless, I had to say a few words of thanks.

Early in December each year we hold a very festive 'Let's Sing it's Christmas' in Stourbridge Town Hall. It has usually been kindly sponsored by HSBC Bank, but in 2005 for some reason they did not do so, so I offered to take their place. Thinking

*Sue and Geoff host a
'tea and cakes' party,
May 2004.*

it through, I thought it would be much more beneficial for Rotary if I used the money to stage another Grand Raffle, which I did. Once again, my directors managed to get help from most of my manufacturers in the form of donations of expensive electrical items so that, together with a BMX bike that I had just won in a raffle, we had well over £2,000 worth of prizes on offer. With the help of all the Rotarians and a couple of days selling raffle tickets in Asda supermarket at Brierley Hill, we raised a total of £3,400. The money was split between two schools for pupils with learning difficulties, namely, Pens Meadow at Wordsley and Sunfield at Clent.

Since being in the club I have had a chance to see just how much the Rotary movement helps not only local and national charitable causes but also overseas ones. It really is a wonderful worldwide organisation of fellowship and caring.

23

Other Charitable Causes

One day, at our usual Wednesday lunchtime meeting of the Stourbridge Rotary Club, one of my fellow members, Councillor Brian Edwards, kindly asked me if I would like to join a charity board of which he was chairman, the Anthony and Gwendoline Wylde Memorial Charity. The Wylde Trust, as it is known, was created under the will of Mrs Wylde, by which funds in the order of £1 million were left in trust, the annual income being distributed to groups and individuals within the areas of Kinver, Stourbridge and south Staffordshire.

I attended my first meeting in January 2000; other board members included fellow Rotarians, Bryan Evers and my friend from the Hospice board, David Johnson. I already had experience of the Wylde Trust at the Hospice, as grants of several thousand pounds had been made during previous years.

On occasions we have to consider an application from an applicant who has already applied to my own trust, the Hope Trust, or the Rotary Club, and in those cases my prior knowledge of the circumstances is helpful. On other occasions I receive an application to my trust from a student, and am able to recommend that they apply to the Wylde Trust, which may be able to help . A large number of people and organisations receive help every year through the generosity and foresight of this Kinver couple.

One of the many charities I have tried to help over the years, and worth a mention, is the Sunfield Children's Home at Clent. I was particularly impressed the first time that Sue and I visited Sunfield. Subsequent visits have endorsed the respect and admiration we have for this residential home for autistic children, as well as for the people who run it and carry out its fundraising.

As well as supporting them in other ways, the Geoff Hill staff competed in their inaugural It's a Knockout competition, held in 2002, with our enthusiastic team called the Geoff Hill Wrinklies (something to do with their ages) and, to our surprise, we won the trophy. To cap it all, when the event was repeated in 2003 we made a late charge from behind and won again, beating the other five competing teams. My staff must all get it from me, and are a very determined lot when it comes to a challenge!

Another local organisation for which I have every respect and admiration is Age Concern, Stourbridge, led by president Derek Elton and chairman, Ron Dalton. Each year they had very kindly invited Sue and me to their Summer Fête, held in the grounds of the old Stourbridge Maternity Hospital, in which they are located. At the fête held in July 2002, knowing that I would be leaving the Hospice the following months they said they would be delighted if I would join their board of management. Tempting as this was, leaving the Hospice was a quite traumatic time for me, and I declined with thanks, taking a few months off to decide in which direction to spend my remaining spare time.

In July 2003 we were again invited to attend, and to join them for strawberries and cakes afterwards. The invitation to join the board was renewed and was also extended to Fred Hunt, a fellow Rotarian, well known as a leader of Dudley Council, and also Millennium Mayor of Dudley. We both accepted the invitation, and looked forward to participating and being able to contribute to this already very well-run organisation.

We successfully negotiated our first fundraising event, which was the 2003 Christmas Fayre, at which we raised a record profit. When we attended our first board meetings, the main item on the agenda was the proposed extensions to the Elton Centre, just off the Ring Road in Stourbridge. Age Concern, Stourbridge, have, in some ways, become a victim of their own success, as the present facilities at the Elton Centre are becoming quite inadequate, and an extensive extension programme is envisaged, at a cost of some £700,000, as soon as funds become available.

When the matter was discussed at the board meetings it was decided that Fred Hunt, with his long-term council experience, would look after any planning issues and that somehow I would be the one to help raise the money to make it all happen.

In the run-up to the 2004 Gala Day in July, I thought it might be a good idea to run a major raffle, similar to the one I had done for the Hospice some thirteen years previously. All my major electrical goods suppliers were invited to donate a suitable raffle prize and by the time I was ready to have tickets printed we had twelve items with a total value of some £2,000. As in the Hospice draw, I provided prizes for people who sold the most tickets, this time a colour television for the winner and a DVD player for the runner-up.

I found this time that it wasn't going to be so easy. I had publicity in the local papers, but whereas for the Hospice we had had a steady stream of people collecting tickets from the shop, this time we didn't get a single soul. The people at Age Concern had said previously how difficult it was to get people to fundraise for them; now I was beginning to see just how difficult it was.

All was not lost, however, as Age Concern sold a lot of tickets themselves and Sue and I were able to get lots of friends and business contacts to help us. After having a good selling session at Asda, Brierley Hill, where we sold over £700 worth, we eventually raised a really worthwhile total of £3,470. I was also able to enlist the staff from Barclays Bank, Stourbridge, to help us on the day and, more importantly, to provide another £750 of matched funding. The weather was kind to us on the Gala Day and the final grand total was a massive £7,370. As the figure is usually in the £2,000s, everyone was quite delighted. Dudley Rotary Club won the television for selling the most raffle tickets.

David Collins, the incoming president of Stourbridge Rotary Club during 2004/5, kindly offered to make Stourbridge Age Concern one of his charities for the year, so we hoped that our Christmas Pâté and Punch would hopefully make

Left to right: Stourbridge Rotarians Norman Burrows, Bob Lloyd-Jones, John Porter and president David Collins, sorting out donated items for the tsunami auction held at Tinkers Cottage in January 2005.

another good fundraising event. The date set for our Pâté and Punch party was 5 January 2005, while our Christmas decorations were still in place. We expected about seventy people: Stourbridge Rotarians and their wives and a couple of directors from Stourbridge Age Concern. The Mayor and Mayoress of Dudley, Councillor Malcolm Knowles and his wife Shirleyanne, also kindly agreed to support us on the night.

We only returned home from a New Year break on 2 January, so didn't have much time to arrange things. The horrendous events of the Boxing Day tsunami in the Indian Ocean were on everyone's minds, so I contacted our Rotary president, David Collins, to see if we could do anything to help the traumatised survivors we were seeing on television each night. It was decided that I should phone all the Rotarians and ask them if they could bring along an unwanted Christmas present or two to auction, and this they did.

After the food was served we had some sixty items to auction, most of which we sold two at a time. At the end of the auction, the Mayor and Mayoress kindly offered another prize of afternoon tea and cakes in the Mayor's Parlour for twelve people. In less than an hour we had raised £900 for the Tsunami Appeal, in addition to the £600 admission money that was to go to Age Concern.

I had received a call from Jeff Jephcott, editor of the News Group newspapers, earlier in the week to tell me that he had been trying without any success to open a charity account for the Tsunami Appeal at a bank, and asking if I could help him. I said that I was pretty sure that I could open one quite quickly under the name of the Geoff Hill Charitable Trust, as I had done for Robert Parsons some four years previously. I phoned my main contact at Barclays Bank, who immediately pulled out all the stops; by the end of the week I had received details of the account, complete with chequebook and paying-in book. The money would go straight into a tax-free investment account and we would be able to claim back an extra 28 per cent Gift Aid from the government on any personal donations made by taxpayers.

Geoff with Pastor Brian Burton from Phuket (centre) and the Revd Peter Jenkins from Amblecote, promoting the Stourbridge News *Tsunami Appeal, 2005.*

We followed up the fundraising that week when Sue and I joined a group of Rotarians to do a collection in the Ryemarket Shopping Centre at Stourbridge, collecting £1,600 in just a few hours. The following Saturday, the presidents of both Stourbridge and Dudley Rotary Clubs organised a day-long collection at Merry Hill, Dudley. At short notice, entertainment was laid on throughout the day, and with the additional help of the other Rotary Clubs in the area, a very rewarding total of £2,900 was raised. On a personal level, I decided straight away to make a substantial donation from personal money that I had put into my charitable trust, deciding to make it £10,000, the same as I had done for Robert Parsons a few years earlier.

I often think up ideas when I wake during the night. On this occasion, I wondered if the £10,000 would be more effective if used to encourage people to put on fundraising events by offering matched funding, to double the amount that they raised. I mentioned this to our Rotary president and he seemed delighted at the idea. He subsequently told me that other Stourbridge Rotarians had also made sizeable donations once they knew what I was going to do. The president of Kinver Rotary Club told me the same, after I had given a talk to their members explaining how the money would be monitored in a tax-free environment, totally free of any charges, for as long as it took.

The money was to be utilised by a Stourbridge pastor, Brian Burton, who for some years had been working as a pastor at Phuket Christian Centre, organising the rebuilding of a school that had been totally demolished. The school was to cost in the order of £250,000 to rebuild. It would house some 200 children, and obviously still more money would be required to equip it. If enough money was forthcoming an orphanage and other projects would probably be undertaken. As Phuket is a popular holiday destination, it would be possible for people who had supported the appeal to see the school for themselves, if holidaying there in years to come.

Fundraising was encouraged by a local pastor, Peter Jenkins, from the Christian Centre in Brettell Lane, Stourbridge, who was in regular contact with his counterpart in Phuket. The News Group printed ongoing details of all the fundraising events that took place each week, ringing me every Tuesday afternoon to get an up-to-date figure of the total money raised. Some ten months later we had £80,000 in the account. It was like the Robert Parsons fundraising all over again.

When I started the Geoff Hill Charitable Trust all those years ago, I had never dreamed of its being used other than to help local needy causes. However, I was very gratified to have it on hand so that local people could help the devastated children who were victims of the horrendous Boxing Day tsunami.

Other Interests

When I was courting my first wife, Lorraine, her sister was a member of Dudley Little Theatre Company, based at the Netherton Arts Centre. I had always been interested in the stage and it was not long before I, too, joined the company. I enjoyed the rehearsals and performances very much and, after some smaller parts, I eventually took over the romantic juvenile lead in *Love on the Dole*, which we performed in March 1950. It was a quite dramatic part that I could really get into, but I don't think my fiancée took very kindly to my love scenes under the old railway bridge!

I also remember performing in a Christmas pantomime when I was cast (some said I was typecast) as Dopey Dick. I was dressed up as an overgrown schoolboy, still in short trousers, and my role was to play to the children in the audience, which was quite fun.

It was while driving home from rehearsals one night and coming down from Dudley towards Brierley Hill, that a police car suddenly cut in front of me and the 'Stop Police' notice lit up in its rear window. The car I was in at the time was my first one, an old 1927 Austin 10, with brakes that were in no way instantaneous. I pressed hard on the footbrake and pulled on the handbrake, but still I couldn't stop in time and had to overtake the police car. When the police car overtook me a second time, I had just about managed to stop. The policeman said that I had been speeding and that I would probably have to go to court.

Sure enough, a few weeks later the summons arrived and I went to court. What happened there was reported in detail in the *Birmingham Post*, and sent to me by a friend. The cutting read:

Unusual plea in Speeding Case – Car that goes with the wind!

Geoffrey Hill, salesman, aged 23, made this assertion at Dudley Court when he said that his car was a very old one and normally would not do more than 30m.p.h., but the road was slightly downhill and there was a very strong following wind that night!

He was fined 20 shillings.

It sounds crazy today, but cars of that era really didn't go very fast, especially when they were as worn out as mine was and I was genuinely trying to make a case for extenuating circumstances!

Acting must run in the family, because my sister, who went out to Uruguay after the war, helped to start the Montevideo Players theatre group with her husband, Colin Fairless OBE, in the early 1950s. Over fifty years later, she still makes the occasional entrance on stage. Both of my nephews out there have also performed over the years.

Some years later I hit on a rather unusual way of trying out my acting skills when on my way to join some friends at a 'tramps ball' in Dudley. I did my very best to look the dirtiest, most horrible-looking tramp that you had ever seen. I had dramatically stained and tore my hat and clothes, then wound some old sacking round my legs, which I tied on with string. Finally, I rubbed coal dust all over my hands and face, then blacked out two of my front teeth with old stage make-up. The object of all this was to knock on the door of my father's house, and see if he could recognise me or not. Half an hour later, adopting a slight stoop, I banged hard on the knocker of The Gables at Brierley Hill.

''Ave yer gorra tanner fer a cuppa tay guvner?' I growled. (A tanner being an old 6d coin.) 'No, I haven't,' was my father's startled reply as he went to close the door even faster than he had opened it. 'Don't be silly dad, it's only me,' I quickly responded, but his 'What do you mean, it's only me!' signified that he still couldn't accept that it was his son he was talking to. He eventually could appreciate that it actually was me, and then broke into laughter which continued for several minutes.

I suppose my other interest was playing golf, and after playing a few municipal courses I joined Blakedown Golf Club in about 1960, when I started my electrical business. I lived in Swiss Drive, Wordsley, at the time and every Sunday morning I used to go off with my friend, Fred Jones from across the road, to play eighteen holes.

My only claim to fame in the few years that we played was when Fred and I fought our way through to the final of the Winter Knockout Foursomes (a competition where competitors play in pairs and take alternate shots). Fred and I had played very well and were one hole up, playing the last hole, so we only needed a half to win the trophy. It was my turn to drive off and I managed to put the ball in the middle of the fairway. All that Fred had to do was put it on the green, which was not too far away, and we were virtually home and dry. Poor Fred. He was a fairly excitable character and the sight of all the members gathering round the last green must have got to him. He took one almighty swipe at the ball and missed it completely! Fred never lived it down, but always took the banter in good heart. Anyway it all ended well because, although we lost that hole, we won the competition on the third extra one, amid many laughs and congratulations.

After a few years playing at Blakedown, I was able to get into the much better and quite handy Enville Golf Club. It was still only eighteen holes at the time, but was soon extended to twenty-seven, and finally made into two separate eighteen-hole courses, as it is today.

The back problems that finished my cycle-racing career persisted when I played golf: I always had to wear a surgical support and take pain-killers before I played. I must have been keen! The steel-ribbed corset that I wore restricted my backswing, but what I lacked in distance I made up in accuracy and I usually went down the middle of the fairway, while my partner's drives were much farther on, but often in the rough. My friends usually decried my drives as 'boring'.

I never won any individual golf championship at Enville, but I did manage to win the inaugural Knockout Snooker Competition. An amusing incident grew around this a few weeks later, when Sue and I popped into the Club House one night after playing a few holes of golf and stayed to watch three good snooker players having a game. Afterwards one of them asked if I played snooker and invited me to make up a four. He then drew me as his partner, and every time I went to play a shot he told me exactly what to do. I potted quite a few balls and, to his surprise, we won the game and the £2 wager. We then played 'double or quits', and guess what – we won again!

It was only then that my partner explained how our opponents played every week in snooker leagues, one of them being runner-up in our big snooker knockout competition. 'I know,' I replied, 'it was I who beat him in the final!' He then swore profusely and afterwards burst into laughter.

Sue took up golf too and, like me, she was determined to give it her best shot. I remember we played in one mixed-foursome competition at Enville when we were both on form, winning by several shots. Unfortunately, it only happened the once.

We had some wonderful times for many years, both on the golf course and at a variety of social events in the evenings, many of which I organised, but it was all to end for both of us when Hospice fundraising came on the scene. When we started putting on fundraising events, opening and running the shops, sourcing and selling all varieties of cards, gift-wrap and other goods, there was suddenly no time left to play golf. In fact, for ten years or so we only took Thursdays off, and even then it was usually 11 a.m. before we left home and we were back again mid-afternoon to make phone calls. For many years we certainly gave it our full-time commitment, and this included weekends too, when needed.

Through all the years of Hospice fundraising everything was done from home: the many board meetings, seeing representatives, stocking and sorting of cards and all the other goods – until a warehouse was finally built at the Hospice, where all the Christmas cards eventually went. All the phone calls were made or received at home or on our mobile phone. Last, but certainly not least, dear Sue was handling all the back-up paperwork and pounding away at the computer in her office, often until 10 p.m. Even some three years after leaving the Hospice, I was still receiving mail delivered to Mary Stevens Hospice, Tinkers Cottage, Lawnswood.

Crazy as it may sound, through all the twelve years of Hospice fundraising, I never had a desk, in fact not even a chair, at the Hospice itself. So when I sold the Christmas cards and said that every penny of profit went to the Hospice, that was exactly what was meant.

25

West Midlander of the Year and the MBE

W hen you are involved in fundraising to the degree that I have been, you are always far too busy to think of rewards. The thanks from beneficiaries and the public at large are more than enough to compensate for the hard slog that is entailed at times.

I remember that, way back in 1993, one of our early day patients at the Hospice gave me a cutting of an article that he contributed to the Halesowen free newspaper, suggesting that I receive some recognition for all the fundraising events I had put on and for the money raised at our first Hospice shop in Stourbridge. Little did he know at the time that I had barely started then.

In 2001 I opened the post one day to find that Sue and I had been invited to a Garden Party hosted by the Queen at Buckingham Palace! Sue, in particular, was very excited and couldn't wait to buy a new dress and hire a hat suitable for the occasion. The big day finally arrived. At 1 p.m. we were parking the car and joining a queue of people that stretched right around the palace. We entered at 2 p.m., walking right through the palace and out to the rear terrace, then down steps to the vast lawns where large marquees had been erected and two bands played alternately throughout the afternoon. Food and drink were served and at 3 p.m. the Queen, the Duke of Edinburgh, Princess Anne and Prince Charles all appeared on the terrace while a band played the National Anthem.

Shortly afterwards the Queen came down the steps and was introduced to people selected at random by the equerries. At one stage she was only a few feet away and I was very impressed to see the amount of time she gave and the obvious interest she showed to everyone to whom she spoke. At the same time the other royals were similarly chatting to people selected from other lines.

We had time to walk around the lovely gardens and lake, the whole proceedings finishing at 6 p.m. We thoroughly enjoyed the afternoon and were surprised and delighted when, at the same time in 2002, we were invited to attend again. This time Sue looked radiant, as usual, but went one better by hiring an enormous bright pink hat. She looked gorgeous.

When the day arrived, we were walking through the crowds around Buckingham Palace before going in, when a couple of ladies from Denmark exclaimed, 'You are the most beautiful person we have seen, may we take your photograph?' Quick as a flash, I replied, 'Certainly, girls. Do you mind if my wife comes on it too?' I don't think they understood my English humour sufficiently to appreciate the joke, but they happily took the photo anyway.

We went through a similar routine to that of the previous year and Sue was a little disappointed at not actually speaking to any of the royals. So we moved over to the line where Prince Charles was talking to some selected couples. As he approached, he couldn't resist stopping and saying to Sue, 'How on earth do you manage to keep that beautiful hat on?' Sue explained in detail how she had had to wrap some material round her head to get a tight fit and then put large hatpins through it to keep it firmly in place. Prince Charles listened intently and had a little chat before moving on. It really made Sue's day!

Towards the end of June 2003 I received a surprise call from ITV Central studios at Birmingham to say that a Judy Owen had nominated me for the award for West Midlander of the Year, which I later discovered was to find the overall Midlander of the Year. They said that they would like to send a film crew over to interview me, and would next Monday, 23 June, at around 2 p.m. be convenient? As you can imagine, it was rather a shock!

The day arrived and Sue and I managed to return home early to prepare ourselves. Dead on 2 p.m. a car pulled into the drive. I went over to it, saying to the man inside, 'Have you come from Central TV to do the interview?' 'No, I'm just the cameraman,' he replied. 'It'll be OK, I'll wait here.' Minutes later another car arrived; this time it was just the 'sound and lighting man'. A few minutes after that a third car arrived and, yes, it was Ed, the man who was actually doing the interview; but we still had to wait a few minutes more for the producer.

Geoff, and Sue wearing her large pink hat, at a Buckingham Palace Garden Party, 2002.

Geoff being interviewed by Ed for ITV Central on being nominated for the West Midlander of the Year award in 2003.

Soon, however, we were all set up. Ed kicked it off by walking past our lovely house, saying that here lived 76-year-old Geoff Hill, who should be now sunning himself on a Caribbean cruise, but instead was still raising money for charity. Afterwards, when he came inside, I outlined to him that my fundraising went back a very long way and started because of my eldest, mentally handicapped daughter, who was in a special residential home at Cannock. I had now been raising funds for forty years. I then came more up to date, explaining about the Hospice shops and lottery that had been so unbelievably successful over the years. It was while I was talking about the shops on camera that Ed suddenly mentioned something that I had told him earlier. I had said that sometimes, if trade was quiet, or if they had something that they thought was really nice and would suit me, I was actually sold items of clothing from the shops.

Anticipating possibility that this would come up, I was wearing a lovely sports jacket purchased only a few weeks previously. Fingering the jacket, I was able to reply, 'Yes Ed, this is one I bought recently – £10 from the Stourbridge Hospice shop.' After he had responded I added, 'Thanks for the free advert!' They all laughed at this, and next day it went out on the 6 p.m. Central News.

I thought at the time that I had done well to get the Stourbridge Hospice shop advertised on television throughout the West Midlands, but when I went into the shop the following week, my friend Rupert was there to greet me with a stern look on his face. 'Fancy saying that on television,' he said. 'You know we only ask £6 or £7 for jackets.' He was quite right of course; I handed over a £10 note at the time because the jacket was 'as new' and very good quality. I did not realise that Rupert would think I was implying that charity shop jackets were dearer at the Stourbridge Hospice shop!

I heard no more for a month or two, and a new contender for West Midlander of the Year was featured on Central News on the last Wednesday of each month. Then, one Thursday in November, a friend told me that all the contenders for the title had been featured on Central News the previous evening. There was a special phone number to ring and seven days in which to phone in your choice.

Next day, when I went into Stourbridge with Sue to do the weekly shopping, I began to realise the wonderful support that my nomination would have from the public. I had got out of my car and walked only a few yards when a dear old lady grabbed hold of me and said, 'You're Geoff Hill, aren't you? I voted for you last night. I've never done anything like this before!' I was to hear a similar message from several other complete strangers over the next few days.

Cedric Grove, the man who made so much money for Robert Parsons at Gornal, went to extraordinary lengths for me when he knew. He actually went canvassing around Kingswinford. Later he told me that over a period of two or three days he had knocked on over 100 doors and to everyone had explained that he would like them to vote for me. They had replied, 'Yes, if it's for Geoff Hill, I will.' He added

Early fundraising days: Geoff practises limbo dancing. In attendance was a sixteen-piece Caribbean steel band, Carruthers, his Great Dane, and wife Sue, 1979. The event raised £650 for his daughter's residential home at Cannock.

that not one had refused. I must say that at the time I was quite amazed at the level of support I received.

On Tuesday the following week, at about 3 p.m., I answered the phone to hear Central Television saying that they had just closed the voting and that I had been nominated a clear winner. They wanted to send a cameraman and interviewer over the following day at 2 p.m. to get my reaction, which would go out on the 6 p.m. Central News that night.

Next day I cut my Rotary lunchtime meeting short so as to be home for 1.45 p.m. – just in time to hear that the cameraman was indisposed and that arrangements were being made to get one over from Telford. He arrived at about 3 p.m. and when the team left, after 4 p.m., to fight their way back to Birmingham through the rush-hour traffic, there was some doubt that they would make it in time. However, they did, and a very abbreviated version made the Central News. I always try to give credit to all the wonderful people who helped me achieve my goals in life, but it was such a long story, and it was inevitable that much of it would be edited out.

At the time it was never spelled out to me by Central Television either how or when I would actually receive the award, but a phone call in January 2004 put all that to rights. The lady who phoned said that there would be a Gala Night on 7 February, when thirteen different Midlander Awards would be presented, together with one for the overall Midlander of the Year, judged by a team of celebrity judges. To get a complete account of my charity work, they planned to send an interviewer and cameraman over for the whole day. She asked where Tinkers Cottage was; it was only when I had difficulty in explaining the way to her that I discovered she was phoning from Carlton Studios in Nottingham, and that the ceremony would be held there, in reputedly the largest television studio in Europe.

A few days later, the interviewer and cameraman arrived, and after spending some time filming and talking to Robert Parsons, they spoke to Judy Owen, the lady who had nominated me. Afterwards they spoke to Sue in her office. For my own interview, they decided that I should sit on our lovely, old, oak staircase. Next, we moved on to the Geoff Hill Electrical Store, where they filmed me walking around both inside and outside the shop. They then interviewed Linda Cartwright, who has been with me for twenty-eight years. She implied that I had been thinking up new fundraising ideas during most of this time. Finally, we visited the Stourbridge Hospice shop, where they chatted to my friend Rupert, as Pat Smith, the manageress, was off work that day. They then drove round to the other five Hospice shops to get shots from the outside, before starting their long haul back to Nottingham.

The big day soon arrived and Judy Owen, Sue and I set off for the hotel where we were staying in Nottingham, while my stepson, Richard, joined us from London. We had a taxi over to Carlton Studios, and walked down the red-carpeted entrance hall just before 6 p.m. We met up with all the other, very interesting, award winners for drinks and a briefing and then, after a more formal champagne reception, we moved into the grand studio for the award ceremony.

After some initial entertainment the host for the evening, veteran Central News presenter Bob Warman, opened the proceedings. For the next 2½ hours we had a chance to see the background to each of our nominations, and then the recipient was presented with the award and said a few words.

My turn was to come towards the end of the proceedings. Shortly before, I asked Sue if she would like to join me on the stage. I think she was a little taken aback at first, but she said that she would love to. When the time arrived the audience saw an edited preview of the film that had been taken a week or so earlier, and then Sue and I made our way through the audience and up to the stage. I explained straight away that I had brought Sue up with me because she had played such a supportive role in all my charity endeavours. I then spoke briefly of all my fundraising activities and my charitable trust, etc. I closed by saying that I thought it was refreshing for a charity worker to be recognised, as it is invariably footballers, rugby players, businessmen or other personalities who get paid big money for what they do anyway. Shortly after that the overall Midlander of the Year, chosen by the team of judges, was announced to be Martin Johnston, the Leicester and England Rugby captain, whose team had recently won the World Cup in Australia!

As the criterion for the award was that the winner should be the person who had done the most during the course of the year to increase the prestige of the Midlands, I knew beforehand that I hadn't a chance of getting it, mine being a very locally based endeavour. What was gratifying to me was learning that in the initial round of the telephone voting I had received 39 per cent of the total vote, with the other six contenders averaging about 10 per cent each. It reinforced to me how the public at large respected someone who had done his utmost to improve (often in just some small way), the lives of his local community.

The award ceremony was subsequently featured on Central News. A few days later an hour-long programme went out, featuring all thirteen winners.

It had been arranged for me to be the speaker, a couple of weeks later, at the Dudley and District Business Club meeting, held at the Copthorne Hotel, where I

was able to address all the other business members on how involvement in charities could help their business. I don't suppose anyone there was ever likely to go to the lengths that I had done. I believe, however, that people do have respect for firms that are not always trying to make lots of money solely for themselves. I tried to get this

Geoff receives ITV's West Midlander of the Year Award from Central News presenter Joanne Malin, 7 February 2004.

message across, and suggested various painless ways that they could try. I also had a chance to officially thank Judy Owen, who at the time was the vice-chairman of Dudley and District Business Club, for so kindly nominating me in the first place.

The following morning I achieved celebrity status when I was invited by Inspector Nigel Perkins, the very community-minded officer in charge of Stourbridge Police Force, to cut the ribbon on a small police facility in the busy underpass which goes under Stourbridge Ring Road to the bus and train station. It was the first of its kind in the country and, as over 100 crimes had been reported there in the previous twelve months, it seemed to be a facility that was badly needed.

Once again, the ITV camera crew and local press were there. I did hear that their original intention had been to try to get Steve Bull, the famous Wolves footballer, to do the honours, but Inspector Perkins had suggested that I, having just been nominated West Midlander of the Year, might be a more appropriate person for this community-based event. Charity fundraisers were suddenly up there as celebrities, along with the football stars. I must be creating a precedent at last!

Unfortunately, as time passed, the police unit appeared to be very seldom in use, and a campaign was started for the underpass to be closed and to be replaced by a pedestrian crossing across the busy Ring Road – a recommendation that I totally agreed with, particularly for the elderly people.

I had just about completed these memoirs and was about to 'put them to bed' for the publishers, when, opening my mail one day, I found among all the bills and junk mail a letter from 10 Downing Street, saying that I was to be awarded an MBE for my outstanding charity work in the Queen's Birthday Honours list!

When I told Sue she was ecstatic. She then explained that for nearly nine years she had been helping different people to try to get this recognition for me, adding that as none of their copious efforts had been successful she had only quite recently decided to admit defeat and put all her files away in a cupboard.

The timing of the award couldn't have been better, because we had eight American couples over from Sturbridge, near Boston, a club with which Stourbridge Rotary Club is twinned. It was the big event of their stay, held at Stourbridge Golf Club on the evening of Friday 11 June, with the Rotary district governor and his wife present, also the Mayor and Mayoress of Dudley. It was about 10 p.m. and, although my MBE was not to become effective until midnight, the incoming Rotary president, David Collins, who lives quite close to me, announced to the 100 or so present that I was to receive this award. Everyone was delighted, and the district governor, who had also been honoured with an MBE, explained especially for our American visitors exactly how respected this award was. Afterwards everyone came over to shake my hand and congratulate me. It was to be the start of two weeks or more of letters, cards (over 100), phone calls and being stopped in the street or supermarket by dozens of ordinary people, who all seemed just as delighted as I was.

The actual day the award was announced in the press, we had arranged for David Collins and his wife to bring their two American guests round to join us and our two American guests for a last dinner party before they went off to Scotland for a week, prior to their returning home. There was a loud knock on our door about

Sue and Geoff with the Mayor of Dudley, Councillor Rosemary Tomkinson, after it was announced that Geoff was to receive the MBE. The photograph was taken at Stourbridge Rotary Club when guests from Sturbridge, USA were present, 11 June 2004.

8 p.m. When we opened it, the ladies were dressed up to the nines, with fake diamond tiaras in their hair, and the men were sporting flash dinner jackets and bow ties. All were bowing, scraping and passing appropriate comments; it was hilarious! Once they came into our house the boys disappeared into another room, reappearing a few seconds later wearing casual shirts in place of their flash gear. It was a great night.

My 77th birthday was on the following Wednesday week, and Sue and I decided to invite people who, over the years, had tried to get me nominated for the award. Unfortunately, several could not come because of holidays or other commitments, but we had nearly thirty there on the night, and once again it was a very memorable one. Judy Owen started by bringing me a bright red football shirt with 'Geoff Hill MBE' on the front and 'HILL 77' as my number on the back! Debbie Bowen, chairman of Dudley and District Business Club, brought me a Thornton's champagne bottle done in dark chocolate, with 'Geoff Hill MBE' in white chocolate on the front, and so it went on. Jeff Jephcott, editor of the News Group newspapers, who had been first to phone me on the day the awards were announced, saying how delighted he was to see the announcement, and who had put a lovely piece about Sue and me in the *Stourbridge News*, came along. Rob Newey, a Kingswinford butcher who, many years ago, was in our Hospice fundraising group, was another guest who, I was told, had worked tremendously hard to help get my award. He didn't know it was my birthday and insisted on coming round the next day with presents of wine and the most beautiful flower arrangement that we had ever seen. Dear Rupert at the Stourbridge Hospice shop was unable to come on the night but, of all things, the day my award was announced happened to be his 80th birthday! He said that when he heard the news it was the best birthday present he could have wished for. We've certainly met some super people on all our charity endeavours.

It was approximately three months later that we received the official invitation to Buckingham Palace. Sue was soon out 'sussing' her new frock, and we were able to let the palace know that our two guests on the day would be my brother, Bob, and Sue's son, Richard; it was all going to happen on Friday 15 October 2004. Coincidentally, the hotel we always stayed at when in London was a small one called the Elizabeth, just across Hyde Park from the palace.

When we arrived the day before the investiture there had been heavy rain during the night, and water had seeped into the lower-ground room we usually have at the hotel. They had, however, found us a very pleasant room on the fourth floor, with a four-poster bed, which turned out to be called the 'Elizabeth Room'. We thought this most appropriate, as we had expected to see the Queen the next day, but when we arrived at Buckingham Palace the investees were told that Prince Charles would be doing the investitures, as the Queen was opening a mosque at Hounslow that morning.

It was a beautiful occasion, in stunning surroundings, and when it eventually came my turn to approach Prince Charles I thought he would probably ask me why I was being honoured that day, but he quite surprised me by saying, 'Are you still doing that wonderful work for the Hospice of yours at Stourbridge?' 'No,' I replied. 'As a matter of fact I have moved on from there. I'm now, probably more appropriately, a fundraising director for Age Concern, Stourbridge, who need to extend their day care facilities there.'

He smiled, we had a short chat and it was all over.

We were at the palace from 10 a.m. until 12.30 p.m., and have some superb photographs and a half-hour film of the whole ceremony, which also showed my guests arriving and leaving the palace. It was a very special and spectacular day.

Prince Charles presents Geoff Hill with the MBE at Buckingham Palace, October 2004.

Sue and Geoff with Sue's son, Richard Morgans, and Geoff's brother, Bob Hill, at
Buckingham Palace after the MBE ceremony in October 2004. (Charles Green)

Later we reflected on how we had been working flat out at fundraising for
umpteen years, when suddenly these two honours had both come my way. There
was more to come!

Sue and I had just returned from Guernsey, where we had been attending a week-
long conference to celebrate 100 years of Rotary. It was only three weeks after
receiving my MBE and we were at the electrical store in the back office collecting

my mail. There, among all the requests to my charitable trust and the odd bill or two, I suddenly saw an envelope from Buckingham Palace! I couldn't believe it at first, because when I opened the envelope I saw that it was an invitation from the Queen to attend a Christmas Reception at the palace on Tuesday 7 December.

Although my dear Sue usually appears more chatty and sociable than me, she often does not relish going out to all the functions to which we are often invited. I thought I would have a bit of fun with this one, so I passed it to my accounts director, Linda Cartwright, to whom Sue was talking, saying nonchalantly, 'Sue is not too keen on going out to all these places all the time, Linda – I don't know if you'd be interested?'

Linda opened the invitation, still talking to Sue. Her eyes suddenly lit up and her jaw dropped as she read it. Sue then realised that it was something pretty special and read it too.

A few weeks later, at 5 p.m. we were driving into the palace again, but this time for a totally different type of occasion. As we walked up the impressively wide, red-carpeted staircase, lined with magnificent Christmas decorations, we could hear a choir above singing carols which seemed to echo all around us. There were four or five large rooms where we could wander around and recline on the wonderful furniture. Drinks and canapés were served all evening to the 200 or so invitees and their guests. From 6 p.m. until 8 p.m. the Queen, Prince Edward and Sophie, his wife, the Duke of Gloucester, the Duke of York and the Duke of Kent, walked among us talking to the people. It was all unbelievably relaxed, which made it all the more enjoyable.

In one of the rooms we were able to talk to the Queen, who asked me what, exactly, I was involved in. I tried to explain quickly that it covered a great deal of ground and just mentioned two or three of the main activities. I think she was quite impressed, and she said something like, 'Good gracious me', before she turned to Sue for a few words and then moved on. Later, we had a chat with Prince Edward, who seemed quite interested and, once again, very relaxed. When Sue thanked him for having us all there, he replied appropriately, 'Well it's big enough, isn't it!'

There were many other charity and community workers there, also Ryder Cup golfers, Ian Botham the cricketer, explorers and film-makers. It was, however, a young blind man standing in the corner of one of the rooms with his wife at his side and his guide dog at his feet to whom I most enjoyed talking that evening. He was certainly the most resilient handicapped person I have ever spoken to, and I was full of admiration for the very positive attitude he had to life. Apparently, he had suffered from a hereditary progressive loss of vision, with which he had eventually come to terms. Over the last few years he had raised over £80,000 for Guide Dogs for the Blind by running (with assistance) in the London Marathon and Great North Run. He also planned to run the New York Marathon in 2005, and was already busy planning a large charity cricket match for 2006. After listening to all this and telling him a little of my fundraising escapades, I said to him, 'Don't you think that fundraising becomes an obsession, Dave?' Straight away he said, 'You're right, Geoff, it does.'

Geoff Hill MBE.

No matter how successful an event or a year's fundraising may be you always want to do better when next year comes around. When we exchanged addresses at the end of our long chat, I learned that he lived at West Bromwich and that the cricket match was to be held at Himley Cricket Club! In February 2005 I unexpectedly received a 'cheeky letter' from Dave, asking if I would act as a sponsor for him in the London Marathon in April 2005. As he wrote in his letter, 'It's not too many people who can say that they have become friends of someone that they met in Buckingham Palace!' He was delighted when I replied that I would be happy to be his sponsor.

Although the royalty retired at 8 p.m., drinks and canapés continued to be served until the last guest left at about 9 p.m. Ours was the last but one car left in the inner courtyard when one of the policemen on duty approached us. Sue said (jokingly), 'I'm afraid the car won't start, officer, I think we'll have to stay here for the night.' He straight away retorted, 'I'm afraid that any cars left here are automatically put through the crusher.' The car then somehow started immediately.

We had often wondered why we were invited back to the palace so soon after my investiture, and it then occurred to me that this invitation had been sent to the electrical store, whereas all the earlier correspondence for the MBE had been addressed to my home. It seems the palace records must show both a Geoff Hill at Tinkers Cottage, Lawnswood, who 'raises all this money' and another Geoff Hill at Amblecote, Stourbridge who, via his charitable trust, 'gives money away'. Actually, Sue and I are both quite happy with this arrangement, so if you are ever invited to the palace please don't give the show away.

Sue was ecstatic for days after our visit to Buckingham Palace and I was particularly delighted, when I looked at the full list of invitees, to see just how many charity and community workers were there. I certainly came away with a lasting impression that people in higher circles are now certainly appreciating the many thousands of people who so willingly give their time and expertise to help others less fortunate than themselves.

Finally, our many thanks again to all the kind people who have helped over the years to make it all happen for us.

26

Heart Attack

In June 2005 I was featured in the local newspapers for something rather different from fundraising – I had a heart attack. On Saturday 4 June at 9 in the morning, Sue was rushing me into the Emergency Unit at Russells Hall Hospital. There it was confirmed by an ECG that I was having a heart attack, and needed an emergency procedure that carried the risk of bleeding internally or even in the brain. I had to sign that I was aware of this possibility, so that the procedure could be started as soon as possible.

Fortunately, a little while later a further ECG was taken, which showed that the heart attack was in remission, so it was classified as a heart attack that had aborted and there was a change of plan. I was taken into the Intensive Care Unit at Coronary Care for 24 hours before being moved into the adjacent ward.

At no time had I experienced any chest pains. For several months I had suffered occasionally from a severe pain in the back of the throat, quite similar to heartburn. In fact, when I first mentioned it to the doctor he prescribed tablets for indigestion. It was only a couple of weeks before the heart attack that this was referred to as angina, and confirmed by a consultant whom I saw just three days before being rushed into hospital. When I saw the consultant and had routine blood pressure and pulse readings taken the nurse had said 'You're spot on. Did you used to be an athlete Mr Hill?' 'I used to be a racing cyclist,' I replied adding 'a long time ago.' 'You'll live for ever!' she exclaimed as I left the room. She should have seen me three days later!

I had thought that it might be a nice idea to have some of the Stourbridge Age Concern people round for tea and cakes while everything was still looking good after our Open Garden, a couple of weeks earlier. Some forty-five people, plus a few carers, had said they would come and the visit had been scheduled for the Monday that I was now in hospital. Obviously, it had to be cancelled at short notice, signs being put up in both Age Concern centres. As Sue was leaving the house to visit me on that Monday an elderly lady was walking up the drive. When Sue asked if she could help her, the lady replied, 'I've come for the tea and cakes in your lovely garden.' Sue told her that the Open Garden had been cancelled, and the reason why, and the lady replied, 'Oh, there are about fourteen others on the way here!' Sue then had to put a sign on the gate saying why the Open Garden had had to be cancelled at such short notice.

Meanwhile, I was in the new Cardiac Unit at Russells Hall Hospital, which had only been open for some four weeks. I was completely out of pain and quite keen to proceed with the angioplasty procedure that would be carried out at New Cross Hospital, Wolverhampton, which had state-of-the-art equipment. I had to wait until 10 p.m. on Thursday to get a bed there. Although I had been fully prepared medically to have the procedure carried out the next day, I was told at about noon that it would have to be cancelled and I would have to wait until the following Monday for it to take place.

Monday rolled around, and at 12.15 p.m. I was being wheeled into the operating theatre. An incision was made in my groin for a small metal frame, called a stent, to be inserted and fed up to a restricted area in one of my main heart arteries. When it was located there, a balloon inside the stent was inflated to extend the metal frame, thus compressing the restrictions in the artery walls and increasing the blood flow. Three of these stents were positioned in two of my heart arteries, but when the consultant tried to locate a fourth one, he found the artery too restricted to get it into place. All this was done under local anaesthetic, which meant that I was able to watch the whole procedure on a large television screen beside the operating table.

It was then decided that, as I had been worked on for nearly 2 hours, it would be best for me to come back again in six weeks' time. When I asked how he would eventually clear the blockage he said that he would use a 'file'. I later checked this out with another doctor who called on me in my room, and he said that it was actually a very small drill. Sounds interesting! I was told, however, that when all the stents were in place, it would be equivalent to my having had a double heart by-pass. Instead of opening my chest, removing my heart and inserting veins from my legs to replace the restricting ones, they would have rejuvenated the arteries in a far simpler operation.

I must say a very big 'thank you' to the many friends and members of the public for the dozens of phone calls that were made to Sue over this period. They came so thick and fast that she had to put the answer phone on for a short time each evening in order to get herself something to eat!

When I was admitted to hospital there had been one or two appointments on the horizon. One was to perform the official opening of a charity shop in a rather underprivileged area in Dudley on Wednesday 15 June. I asked Sue to phone Deb Brownlee and tell her that, unfortunately, I would not be able to fulfil the engagement. Deb replied that she would not get a substitute, but would put off the grand opening until I felt better!

The second appointment was to open Stourbridge Carnival on Sunday 26 June and although I had only been out of hospital for about ten days (I was told to stay around the house for the first two weeks!), I was just about able to make it to this one. It was a most beautiful day weather-wise, with huge crowds everywhere, and guaranteed to be a most successful event – which is always nice to see, because so many months of work come to nothing if the heavens open on the day.

I would like to thank all the 100 or so people who sent me get-well cards. Most were telling me to just 'slow down a bit'. I'll try, but it won't come easily, I'm sure.

Six weeks later I was back at New Cross for the second operation, which I expected would not take very long to perform. However, the surgeon had difficulty clearing the artery and fitting the stent, which again meant a 2-hour operation. Back in my en-suite bedroom the surgeon visited me and apologised for the long time it had taken, explaining that it had been quite complicated, but that he had eventually achieved the desired result. For this I thanked him.

It was probably an hour or so later that I started vomiting and brought back all the food and water that I had consumed in my bedroom. Not long after that, I vomited again, but this time it was blood coming up, which Sue had to catch in a papier-mâché bowl. This continued at regular intervals, so I was connected up for a blood transfusion. I also had a swelling of my right thigh, which was due to blood escaping where the incision had been made for my operation. This necessitated a doctor and a male nurse massaging the thigh to disperse the build-up of blood. I suddenly seemed to be in quite a state, eventually going in and out of consciousness. Poor Sue, who remained constantly by my bedside during the night, was naturally getting extremely worried as she kept collecting bowls of vomited blood. This went on most of the night, until eventually it stopped.

The surgeon had stayed quite late and was back again to assess me early the following morning. For the next three days I was wired up to an ECG, but when a doctor came round late on Friday morning I explained that I would prefer to go home, as very little else could be done for me there over the weekend. They wanted to insert an endoscope down my throat to inspect the area where all the blood had escaped, but I said I could return as an outpatient to have that procedure carried out. He eventually agreed. Sue was, naturally, very relieved to have me home again,

Geoff at the opening of the Stourbridge Carnival, 26 June 2005.

although at the same time worried that, knowing me, I might have talked my way out too soon.

A few weeks later I made contact with Action Heart in their wonderful new facility at Russells Hall Hospital, Dudley. Partners are encouraged to attend all the exercise regimes and also to attend a whole variety of seminars on drugs, exercise, food, stress, etc. Neither of us can speak highly enough of the wonderful attention and facilities that we have had for our hour-long exercise programme three times per week. We both are now so much fitter, and in my case the problems that I had for years attributed to a leaking mitral valve in my heart were now largely rectified by the insertion of the four stents in the blocked arteries. It may sound crazy but, in retrospect, really the best thing that happened to me in 2005 was to have a heart attack.

We are now able to show appreciation for their wonderful service by accepting an invitation to join their fundraising team. Our first task with the group has been to produce a highly saleable calendar for 2007. I was also belatedly able to add Action Heart to the list of recipients from the sale of the 1,000 books I hope to sell.

I was later able, belatedly, to open the charity shop at Kates Hill, Dudley, which I had helped a little in its early days. Afterwards I was also able to give a talk for an hour that they had requested me to give on my varied life activities. They, in turn, very kindly presented me with a certificate making me an honorary member of their Young at Heart Group. Quite a novel title, I thought. I'll try to live up to it.

During October I got my directors at the Geoff Hill Store to approach manufacturers for raffle prizes and I then spent most of November selling all the raffle tickets (with Sue's help). With the assistance of Stourbridge Rotary Club as well, we raised a final total of £3,400.

My fundraising was now back in business!

27

In Conclusion

I think we all start out in life wondering what the future holds in store for us. Then, as years go by, we chop and change direction in our minds as to what sort of career or lifestyle to pursue. Some, like my son Nigel, opt out of regular society to pursue world travel as a 'free spirit', which he has done for most of the last twenty years. Much as I love travelling and exploring different countries, my main focus in life has always been seeing and accepting challenges, and trying to fulfil them to the best of my capabilities. Fortunately, I have usually been reasonably successful, which has meant that I have had a wonderful lifestyle in a gorgeous house and grounds, also with an idyllic place of our own to escape to in Wales.

The money for this and anything else that I may wish to do has mainly been earned from the forty-five years in my electrical store. Taking that statement one stage further brings me to all the many thousands of people who have supported my store – in some cases for most of those forty-five years. Yes, it's true, because when I meet them they love to tell me when they purchased their first appliance, just what it was and, sometimes, even how much it cost!

This brings me to the fact that I feel I owe a debt of gratitude to the local community, particularly as I have had such a personal relationship with all of my customers. This, to me, is a very good reason for the unstinting commitment to all the fundraising extravaganzas that Sue and I have undertaken during the last fifteen years. I couldn't have done anything like as much without Sue's wonderful help and support over the years, and her attractive personality has always made everything so enjoyable. Finally, for the mammoth fundraising carried out for Mary Stevens Hospice, a very big 'thank you', and it was great having your loyal support, to all the 25 staff and 130 or so volunteers who helped in the Wordsley fundraising group, the Hospice shops and the lottery.

Over all the years my own staff at the Geoff Hill Electrical Superstore have been absolutely wonderful. It has been particularly rewarding to me, after having left the day-to-day running of the business, to receive wonderful praise for them from people I meet on almost a daily basis.

Having had such a privileged life myself, I feel it only right to try in some small way to help others who have been less fortunate. I am already expanding the Geoff Hill Charitable Trust with my own money and will continue to do so over the years, to try to help many more people who are not as blessed as I have been.

My life started in a very basic but happy home in the old industrial Black Country. Over the years I was never afraid to work as many hours of the day, or night, as I felt were needed to improve my lot.

I have never been one to conform rigidly to business practice and have been prepared to follow my own intuition, having a go at any activity or fundraising extravaganza that came into my head.

To sum it all up, I guess, as Mr Sinatra so famously sang, '. . . and through it all – I did it my way'!

The Geoff Hill Charitable Trust at 7 High Street, Amblecote, Stourbridge, DY8 4DE, is always very appreciative of any financial help. If you are a taxpayer, the trust can obtain an extra 28p for every £1 donated by Gift Aid – Geoff, Sue and the assistant who types all the trust correspondence don't take out a penny for expenses. All the money goes to local needy causes.